The Cleavers Didn't
Live on Our Street

The Cleaver's Didn't Live on Our Street

✦

Growing up in Windsor, Ontario in the 1940's and 1950's

J.V. Trott

iUniverse, Inc.
New York   Bloomington

The Cleaver's Didn't Live on Our Street
Growing up in Windsor, Ontario, in the 1940s and 1950s

iUniverse books may be ordered through booksellers or by contacting:

iUniverse
1663 Liberty Drive
Bloomington, IN 47403
www.iuniverse.com
1-800-Authors (1-800-288-4677)

*Because of the dynamic nature of the Internet, any Web addresses or links
contained in this book may have changed since publication and may no longer be
valid.*

ISBN: 978-1-4401-9961-5 (sc)
ISBN: 978-1-4401-9963-9 (dj)
ISBN: 978-1-4401-9962-2 (ebk)

Printed in the United States of America

iUniverse rev. date: 12/22/2009

To the memory of Sylvia (a.k.a. Suzie) and for all the family who remain and those who have gone before.

Special thanks to my daughters Rebecca and Christine and my friend Clay Lafleur for their assistance in the preparation of this book.

Epigraph

Life is a comedy for those who think but a
tragedy for those who feel.

Horace Walpole

Get your facts first, and then you
can distort them as much as you please.

Mark Twain

Best Wishes

Enjoy

John

16/06/2010

Contents

Introduction

My father believed there was no such thing as a bad job. In the 1940's, Windsor, Ontario was an industrial and manufacturing city, a mile wide river south of Detroit, Michigan. It was here where I grew up. Here where I watched as my father and uncles donned uniforms and headed off to war and then returned to make their livings on assembly lines. Just as the current generation put their faith in the stock market and big banks, so in the 1940's and 50's, did we believe that what was good for General Motors was also good for us. Sometimes it was and when it wasn't good enough, it was here where I waited on the sidelines watching as my father and mother spent the hot days of summer picking tomatoes so that we could make ends meet while the assembly lines shut down to save the automakers money.

Perhaps the biggest change during these years was the coming of television. It impacted our leisure time and shaped our values just as the computer and the Internet do today. In those days, shows such as "The Nelsons," "Father Knows Best," and "Leave It to Beaver," created an idyllic picture of life in suburbia. We lived in the sticks and were for a long time without a refrigerator, furnace, telephone or family car. We were from the other side of the tracks where father didn't always know best and the Cleavers never came to visit.

This is not an autobiography but rather a book about family in all its fun and dysfunction. It is a collection of family fictions based on what Mark Twain called a "fact" or "particle of truth." I have followed his advice and distorted these kernels as dictated by my imagination.

I recommend the writing process to anyone who wishes to recapture the everyday memories of years gone by and share them with loved ones and others living through similar and seemingly mundane experiences that indeed, form the fabric of our lives. I wrote the first story "Presents in a Christmas Past" more than two years ago. It is a story about my favourite time of year, Christmas, and my favourite person, Sylvia–or Sib, as I called her. Although my sister has been gone for almost 15 years, I found that I could still not write her name into the stories and so she became Suzie. As I rediscovered Suzie and Christmas, other people and incidents came crowding in: uncles, aunts, cousins, friends, neighbours, and of course, mother and father.

The stories are arranged according to themes and so they skip back and forth through the 1940's and 1950's. The times shifts are small and I hope, not too distracting. They were years of transition during and following the war, characterized by boom and bust; layoffs and strikes; overtime and bonuses. Although there may be parallels between these times and the times we live in today, these stories do not pretend to offer any magic solutions or identify any significant tipping points. Rather they provide insights into eternal enigmas such as building a Christmas tree from scratch; inviting a drunken Santa to spend Christmas Eve with the kids; celebrating Thanksgiving with your best friend on the menu; or taking driving lessons in a garbage truck.

In preparing these stories I found a linkage between the generations and the troubled times we all live through. Somewhere in the writing process my grandparents wandered once again over the Lake Erie beach for a family reunion, and the antics of my granddaughter, Hazel, took shape as "Suzie's First Word." The story "Disorganized Play" developed as I watched my five-year-old grandson, Matthew, and his peers attempt to come together as a team on the soccer and T-ball fields.

And so it is that the writing has joined more than a hundred years of family history. Now that I'm the grandfather at the party, I don't intend to wander away in search of bottles as my grandfather did; I'd rather stay and join in the play.

My life and writing have left me with two truths: the value of family and the importance of humour. Hopefully both with shine through on the pages that follow.

Chapter I

My Best Friend Suzie

My sister was two years younger than me, and we grew up together. This chapter describes her first word and a memorable Thanksgiving and Christmas.

◆　　◆　　◆

Suzie's First Word

Growing up I had a younger sister who would become my best friend. But not right away. I was about three when my mother told me our family was going to get something very nice and very soon. And I can tell you that I was pretty excited. What could it be, I wondered? A car, a swing-set or maybe one of those radios with a picture like I'd seen in the hardware store. I could hardly wait for the surprise to arrive. Well, mother went away for a few days and came back with a small, red, crying thing in a pink blanket. It turned out to be my sister.

Her arrival sure changed things in our house. Everybody thought she was great. They made a big fuss over her. Pretty soon the house was full of people and presents. Most of the presents were for the "pink blanket". Every time I turned around, someone was tripping over me to get to her room. My mother wanted me to go in and see her, and so I did. I must say that she wasn't that much. By the time I went in to visit, she wasn't quite as red as before, but she cried a lot, and didn't smell that great either. Mother said she would grow out of that.

After a while, she didn't smell anymore, but she still cried. She could cry at the drop of a toy. Father said it was a "woman thing."

It's a pretty big deal in a family when a baby says its first word. I guess that's because, up until then, they don't do much except eat, sleep, smell bad and cry.

Everybody in our house seemed to go crazy as the time got close. Would it be da, da, da, momma or nanna? Well, as they say, it was none of the above. As soon as father came home from work, he would pick Suzie up and repeat "Da, da, da." At first, Suzie took one look at him and started crying. Once she got used to him, she stopped crying and would just stare.

Then one day, father thought he had a breakthrough. He called out in excitement, "Look dear! Suzie's smiling at me. I think she's going to say, 'Da, da, da.' "

Mother took a quick look and answered, "It's just gas dear. I'm sure it's just gas."

Smiling, Suzie didn't say a thing, but noises did come from below. It was just gas.

Mother had been the first one in the competition. Whenever Suzie was crying mother would rock her and repeat, "Mum, mum, mum." You could tell that she wanted that to be Suzie's first word. Suzie would stop crying and look up at her. But she never uttered the magic word.

Even my beloved grandmother got into the act. While holding Suzie, she would be saying, "Nana, nana." All these adults talking baby-talk, and Suzie just doing her own thing.

Suzie's thing was mostly eating, pooping, crying and grabbing my toys.

"They're mine! Can you get her to stop?" I complained.

"Now dear, don't get upset. She just wants to be your friend. There are a lot of toys - enough for both of you." And that became mother's answer.

"But she always wants the one *I'm* using. They're mine, you know!" I repeated in frustration.

And that's the way it went. In her attempts at friendship, Suzie was into all my stuff. Who wanted a pest for a friend?

When I asked if we could trade Suzie in for a real friend, like a puppy, mother said, "No."

Whenever I complained, she just said that Suzie was part of the family and we weren't taking her back. So, we played together on the floor in a sporadic truce.

Naturally we developed different roles. With my trucks and bulldozers, I was in the construction business. Suzie was much more into destruction. I was the builder of castles, towns and houses. Suzie was the wrecker. One sweep of her chubby hand and flailing arm and another city crumbled to the floor. Suzie turned my car races into demolition derbies. When I told mother that we should call her "Wrecker," she said it wasn't an appropriate name for a girl. So, we stuck with Suzie.

It was during one of those chaotic play periods that Suzie uttered her first word. As usual, she was very busy doing her thing. She had just destroyed two towns, taken the wheel off a police car, and attempted to swallow the officer that went with it. When I tried to retrieve my favorite dump truck from her closed fist, her eyes bugged out and she uttered her first word. "Mine."

She seemed to like it a lot because she repeated it as she clutched the toy to her chest. "Mine, mine, mine."

In amazement, I yelled, "Hey mother, come quick. Suzie's talking."

Mother rushed into the room, her eyes sparkling in anticipation. She asked, "What did she say?" Was it 'mum, mum, mum,' or 'da, da, da?' What did she say?"

But now Suzie wasn't saying anything. She just looked up and displayed a fistful of truck. Even at that young age, I think she knew actions spoke louder than words.

Perplexed, my mother commented, "She's not saying anything now. Are you sure she spoke?"

I smiled and said, "She did. Watch. I'll show you."

I moved in close and tried to twist the truck back.

"Mine, mine, mine," rang throughout the room before Suzy turned on the tears.

Eventually, Suzie did learn how to say "mum, mum, mum" and "da, da, da" and even "nana." But not before everyone had heard more than enough of "mine, mine, mine."

◆　　◆　　◆

Suzie Meets Santa

Christmas is for kids. However, many adults derive their own pleasure from watching a child's anticipation and enthusiasm for the season. I was seven and my sister Suzie was four when she discovered the wonder of Christmas. She involved all the adults around her in its magic. It was mother, who got the Christmas-ball rolling with the gift of the advent calendar. After that it was all downhill. For Suzie, the Christmas snowball took on a life of its own—rolling faster and growing bigger all the way to December 25th.

Holding out the calendar mother said, "Now Suzie, this is a special calendar. We open a little window every day. When they are all open it will be Christmas—Jesus' birthday. Help me open the first window."

Mother guided Suzie's chubby finger to the first flap. They flipped it open and Suzie scooped out the candy inside. Mother smiled, "Well, isn't that a surprise! What do you say Suzie?"

Mouthing the candy, Suzie grinned, displayed a row of small brown teeth and said, "Chocolate."

Seizing the teaching moment, mother prompted, "No, Suzie, what's the magic word?"

Suzie smiled back and said, "More, more."

That's the way it was with Suzie. If something was good, then more was better. And the advent calendar fit right in with her thinking. Mother explained that Jesus got presents on his birthday, and that we would get presents on Christmas day when all the windows were open. I'm not sure how much she understood about the birth of Jesus, but Suzie knew right away that there was a candy behind every window.

The next morning when mother asked to see her calendar, Suzie held it out proudly and announced, "Christmas now. It's Christmas now."

Actually, it was only December 2nd, but when you looked at her calendar, you knew what she meant. All the windows were open and all the candies were gone. Suzie had arranged for Christmas to come early. Mother thought it was funny so Suzie got another calendar, but mother kept that one in her room and supervised the window openings.

The advent calendar had done the trick and Suzie was caught up in the Christmas countdown. Before the introduction of television, there was less opportunity for full-blown commercialization. Nevertheless, radio did its best to fill the void. It carried short Christmas spots and advertisements promoting gifts, Christmas trees, foods and special events. Suzie would listen intently and clap her hands with glee each time the word Christmas was mentioned. The air waves hummed with Christmas music all day long. Mother explained that these special songs were played only once a year and were called carols. Suzie started to call them "Santa songs." Everyone thought she was *so cute*.

Certain songs captured her imagination. Her favorite that year was "Frosty the Snowman." Whenever it snowed, we would go out and build a "Frosty." She knew all the words and was very careful about dressing the snowman properly. Father supplied the corn cob pipe and there was plenty of coal for a button nose and two eyes. The big problem lay in finding a magic hat. Suzie tried endless possibilities. Our snowmen were outfitted in hockey toques, baseball caps, a battered sombrero and father's African pith helmet. Once she tried out the small, veiled pill box that mother wore to church. Even Suzie knew she had gone too far when mother told her that kind of bad behavior led to no visits from Santa. After that, Suzie stuck with the Toronto Maple Leaf toque. Nothing worked. Despite her best efforts, there was no magic in any of the hats and our Frosty never came to life.

Then it was time for the Santa Claus parade. I had been before, but this was Suzie's first time. Once again she emerged as the star of the show. Our parade began at Jackson Park, wound its way down Quellette Avenue towards the Detroit River and ended at Smith's department store. The store would be Santa's home for the next three weeks. We got to the parade late, and I was so far back that I couldn't see much. From her vantage point on my father's shoulders, Suzie had the catbird seat. She began to supply a play by play for my mother and me.

She would call out,: "There's an elf; here comes a clown; or it's Mother Goose and all her friends." Suzie could see and be seen. She got several candies from the marchers.

Finally, Santa arrived and Suzie squealed. "Hi Santa, hi Santa. I'm Suzie, do you remember me? I'm coming to see you soon."

Once again, it was all about Suzie and she knew it.

The next Saturday we did go to Smith's for our visit. You entered Santa's home through a large candy cane entrance. Inside, the room was laid out like Santa's workshop. In the early 1950's even Santa was a stickler for organization. The toys were arranged with girls' toys on one side and the boys on the other. The smaller toys were displayed first and, then, the larger and more expensive. It seemed that the elves had studied 'Marketing 101'. There was a long, slow line snaking its way to Santa's chair. None of the kids complained because it was a good chance to check out the toys and make last minute adjustments to your list.

Suzie had memorized her list and kept repeating, "Barbara Anne skating doll and buggy, Pumpkin Head puppet, a playhouse and one orange cat." She was more than ready.

When our turn came, mother suggested that I go up with Suzie in case she was afraid. An elf handed us two candy canes. Suzie waved the elf away, climbed up on Santa's knee and began, "Hi Santa. My name is Suzie and I've been very good. Do you know what I want for Christmas?"

Then she ran through her list without stopping for a breath.

Santa listened and responded, "Ho, ho, ho! That's good. I know you Suzie. Who is that with you?"

Suzie looked at me from her privileged position and said, "That's my brother, John."

Santa asked with a smile, "Has your brother been good, too?"

Suzie wrinkled her brow, scrunched her eyes and answered, "No, not all the time."

Santa frowned, "Not all the time? What does he do that's so bad?"

Suzie knew this was a chance for payback and said, "Sometimes he won't let me play with his toys."

Santa gave me a hard look. For a second, I thought he was going to take back my candy cane. Then he said, "Now John, you're a big boy. You must look after your sister and always share your toys."

Betrayed by a four-year-old, I studied my shoes and muttered, "Yes sir."

After that, Suzie and Santa had a fine old chat while the elf and I looked on. She reviewed all of her items. Santa was so taken with her that he never did ask me what I wanted.

As we were leaving he pointed a warning finger and said, "Now, be a good boy, John."

Thanks to Suzie, that was a wasted visit for me. I figured I'd better try a write-in campaign. If I could get my cub master to vouch for me, I might still be able to salvage something. The visit had filled Suzie with such confidence that she strutted around like Santa was her uncle from far away.

She was having a great introduction to Christmas; first mother and the advent calendar, and then the one-on-one with Santa. I didn't see how it could get any worse. It was at that point that father decided to get into the act.

One night, at supper, he turned to mother and said, "You know, Suzie really seems to be enjoying the Christmas season. I'd like to do something special for her this year."

Since mother had started the whole countdown thing, he figured she would be receptive.

"Well Jack Hayward mentioned that he had a Santa outfit and he's making appearances at the Legion and the Lion's club. He said he would like to drop by and visit the kids when he finished," father enthused.

Pursing her lips, mother said, "I don't know about that. It sounds a bit risky with Jack."

Father responded, "Now dear, Jack's a bachelor. Doesn't have any family. He just wants to be around some kids at Christmas. He'll be fine."

Still skeptical, mother answered, "I'm not so sure. I only met Jack twice at the Legion, and he wasn't fine either time."

Father continued to argue, "Listen dear, Jack said he would visit us last. He'll have had plenty of practice by then and he won't stop long."

Mother was so caught up on Suzie's Christmas that she weakened. "All right, if you think it's okay. Go ahead and invite Jack."

Suzie and I were very excited when father told us that Santa was going to pay us a personal visit. Mother said we could stay up because he would arrive after our usual bed time. Of course, Suzie was jumping at a chance to renew conversation with her old friend Santa. As for me, I saw this as an opportunity to get back in his good books. I'd been especially good about sharing since the trip to the department store. Besides, I intended to get to him *before* Suzie could say anything bad about me. Everyone was prepared for a big night. We just didn't know how big.

It was about 9:30 when we heard the tinkle of bells at our door. Father opened it and said with a smile, "What a surprise! Look who's here kids. It's Santa. Welcome Santa, come right in!"

Santa was a really big guy. He wavered a bit and bumped into the door jamb as he entered. He managed a gurgled "Ho, ho, ho" and shook hands with father. Father gave Santa a quizzical look and then, taking a firm grip on his shoulder, guided him to the big easy chair. Mother backed away and began shaking her head.

Trying to take control, father said, "Here Santa, maybe you should sit down for a while. You look a bit wobbly. Are you tired?"

Santa slumped into the chair and, peering about, said, "Busy night Johnny. Old Santa had a busy night. The boys at the Legion and the Lion's treated old Santa very well. Where're the kids?"

Seeing my big chance, I moved right in and piped up, "Hi Santa, I'm John and I've been sharing my toys just like you told me. Everybody says I've been very good, and I even have a letter from my cub leader."

Santa reached out for me but somehow just missed making contact. He fixed me with an unsteady look and said, "That's fine Johnny. I never forget the good boys."

Santa smelled kind of funny so I backed away. Suzie headed straight for his lap and she almost made it. As she closed in, Santa began a slow, downward slump and slid nose first onto the carpet.

Suzie ran to his side crying, "Santa, Santa!"

Looking up to mother she asked, "Mother, is Santa dead?"

Mother smiled sweetly and then said, "No dear. Santa is just sleeping. And it's time that you and John went to bed, too."

At next morning's breakfast, the silence between mother and father hung as heavy as a three-day blanket of snow. Then, Suzie came rushing in.

"Where's Santa?" she asked. "Didn't he sleep over?"

Mother broke the silence and said, "No Suzie. Santa had to go back to the North Pole."

Suzie looked puzzled, "That's too bad. I thought of a few more things I would like. I was going to make him cookies and milk for breakfast. Will Santa be coming back?"

Mother gave father a long, hard look and said, "Yes dear. Santa's coming back on Christmas Eve when we're all asleep. But I'm afraid that there will be no more personal visits from Mr. Claus at our house."

And there never were.

◆   ◆   ◆

Suzie and the Goose

It was a big deal when Suzie started school. Mother said she was lonely when we all left in the morning, but she was always smiling when she waved goodbye. That was the year father suggested we go to the market to get ready for Thanksgiving. Mother said she wasn't certain that was a good idea.

"I don't know," she argued. "We'd have to take the bus and then the errands at the market. I'm not sure about the kids. Would you two be good on the bus and at the market?"

There were no stupid children in our family, and my sister and I smiled, and nodded angelically. Truth be told, Suzie and I still fought over the window seat. Being older and bigger, I won ninety percent of the time. When I won, the waterworks would start. That girl could cry at the drop of a pin even if you weren't sticking her with it. She never drank that much either, and to this day, I don't know where all those tears came from.

Mother always rescued her, "Now look here young man, you can be fair and take turns sharing the seat, or you can be a gentleman and give Suzie the seat all the time."

Suddenly the tears stopped and were replaced by a smirky smile. I cast my vote for fair sharing, and we set off for the market. Suzie got first shot at the window seat.

Mother soon had us organized and she said, "Now dad, why don't you and John look at the animals and such. Suzie and I will visit the handicrafts."

I had the feeling there was a plan afoot, but father smiled and said, "Okay, we'll meet you back here in an hour."

He grabbed my hand and led me through the crowd. Although we didn't go often, father loved the market. The sights, sounds and smells took him back to his days on the farm.

In the late 1940's there were live animals as well as fruits, vegetables and meats on display. Vendors had varieties of fish swimming in tanks, puppies and kittens, small pigs, lambs and all kinds of poultry. Going to the market with father was like being escorted through the zoo by the chief zookeeper.

He pointed and said, "See these turkeys, son? They are the ugliest and dumbest creatures on the planet. Even a mother couldn't love that face. Look at that big, ugly wattle hanging down. Looks like it came from another bird by mistake. If they gotta have wattles, they should put them in a less conspicuous place. Too dumb to come out of the rain and they don't even taste good."

Father sure had a hate on for turkeys, but he continued, "Want to see a smart, clean animal? Look at these little pigs. Some people have them as pets and teach them all kinds of tricks. Smart as a whip and cute as a button. Let's get some kielbasa and peameal bacon on a bun. It'll put hair on your chest."

As a boy who was born, raised and worked on a farm, father never let smart and cute get in the way of his appetite. I took a large bite of the kielbasa and a strange taste swam through my mouth, threatening to back up into my nose. I swallowed hard and fast. I was young and didn't know the ingredients. In later years, when I found out, I swore off that stuff forever. People say it's an acquired taste. Before going to bed that night, I checked but did not discover any chest hairs.

Without warning father came to an abrupt military halt.

"Well, look at that! Did you ever see anything nicer?"

I followed his eyes and saw a farmer standing before a stall of small white geese.

"That's just the ticket. Just what we need. How much for that smaller one?"

After fifteen minutes of haggling, they agreed on a price with minimal hard feelings. A survivor of the depression, my father never paid asking price, and liked nothing better than a bargain.

"Where's your car?" the farmer asked.

Father answered, "No car. We came on the bus."

The farmer gave us a quizzical look and said, "Okay, it shouldn't be a problem. She was hand raised and is used to people. I'll give you a cord to bind her feet and you can cover her head with this cloth if she gets nervous. Really, she should be fine. You got a real bargain mister."

Father smiled as if he had invented the bird. He had bought a goose and got a cord and cloth for free.

He was beaming when he said, "Well, isn't that something? Won't your mother be surprised?"

I was pretty sure she would be surprised. I knew I was.

Sure enough when we met up with mother and Suzie, they were both sporting new hats. As usual, mother's plan had worked.

"Well, what do you think? Do you like our new hats?" She stopped herself in mid-sentence and asked, "What on earth is that?"

You could tell by his face that father was extremely proud of his surprise.

"Why, it's a goose dear. And we're taking it home."

Suzie burst forth and grabbed father in as big a bear hug as she could manage.

She exclaimed, "Thank you, thank you, father. It's wonderful!"

Looking a bit perplexed, he simply said, "You're welcome."

Mother and father sat behind us on the bus and discussed their shopping experiences. The goose sat between Suzie and me. She stroked it and talked to it all the way home. The goose seemed to enjoy the attention. Soon the two of them were engaged in spirited, if unintelligible, conversation. I got the window seat.

After we got home, the goose was ensconced in an old cardboard appliance box inside the shed. Suzie appointed herself attendant in charge of feeding and watering. Within two days she was walking the goose around the backyard, and making sure it didn't get into the garden.

It wasn't long before news of our goose spread throughout the neighbourhood. Suzie became its chief herald at school. Soon we were getting daily updates at the dinner table.

"Guess what, mother? I told Mrs. Jamieson about our goose today."

Mother looked up and smiled. "That's nice dear. What did she say?"

Mrs. Jamieson was Suzie's grade one teacher, and although she had only been in school a few months, my sister was ready to nominate her teacher for sainthood. I had been in her class a few years before, and I thought she was okay (but not up to sainthood caliber). As nice as she could be, she did have a thing about talkative young boys. As a result, I got to speak with her a lot–mostly after school.

Suzie continued to roll on, "Oh mother, she thought it was very special. She said that geese are very important and then read us a story from Mother Goose. We're going to hear more stories about geese tomorrow."

Thus began our introduction to "gooseology." On Tuesday, Mrs. Jamieson read them the story of the goose that laid golden eggs. When she asked me, I told Suzie I was doubtful that geese could do that, but that it wouldn't hurt to keep checking. After that, the poor creature hardly ever had a chance to sit down.

"Guess what everybody?" Suzie began every conversation with that phrase but one never had to guess because she quickly revealed the news before you could even open your mouth.

"Mrs. Jamieson read us the story about a goose that saved the village by quacking loudly when the bad guys were coming. I bet our goose could do that. I bet he could be a watch goose, couldn't he?"

Since none of us had considered the possibility, it was hard to know what to say. Mother and I nodded while father undertook a concentrated and detailed examination of his mashed potatoes.

"It was a great story about the village," she continued. "Very exciting! And guess what? Tomorrow Mrs. Jamieson said we could have a class vote to name the goose. Isn't that exciting?"

That darn Mrs. Jamieson never could let up on anything or anyone once she got you in her sights. Father must have found something unusual in the potatoes because he didn't even look up. As it turned out, the goose was named Gerald. When she asked me, I told her it seemed like an okay name. In fact Gerald the Goose had kind of a snappy ring to it.

So that's the way it went for the next week. After school I would play imaginary baseball games by bouncing balls against the wall and fielding rebounds. Games in which the Tigers always won, something they didn't do in the American League. Suzie would be walking Gerald in the backyard and trying to teach him to bark. She kept checking three or four times a day but, great as Gerald was, he couldn't lay a golden egg. It didn't matter to Suzie. She talked my ear off. It was Gerald this and Gerald that. I became her closest confidant even though I didn't see Gerald as a wonder goose. She was happy and there were no more waterworks.

On Saturday Suzie went to spend the day with the cousins. I grabbed my glove and joined an all day pick-up ball game. Being totally free, hanging out with friends, playing a game I loved, that's what Saturdays meant to me. That day was a gold standard Saturday, for awhile, anyway.

When I got home, my mother was busy working at the kitchen table. She was pushing stuff into a pillow case.

"Hey we won, isn't that great? What are you doing?" I was totally mystified.

"I'm making a nice soft pillow out of these feathers," she responded.

"Where did you get them?' I asked. "These aren't Gerald's are they?"

Now she seemed very intent on her work. She nodded and kept stuffing.

"Hey, where is Gerald anyway?" I asked, my voice rising.

Again, without looking up, she nodded to the roasting pan on the cupboard.

"He's gone," she said.

I lifted the lid and peeked in. Gerald was indeed gone. "What are you going to tell Suzie?" I asked.

"Well, I guess we'll just say that he's gone. After all, that's the truth," she answered still looking down.

It was the truth alright but a pretty hard one. Mother broke the news to Suzie when she got back from the cousins. My wonderful Saturday came to a crashing conclusion as her waterworks resumed. Although it was dark and I knew better, I took a flashlight and together Suzie and I searched the backyard. I felt like a Nazi agent or one of those crooked gamblers in the Western matinees. I was the classic traitor, and I didn't like it one bit. Before bed, I told her that we could make posters in the morning. She felt a little better, but I had visions of myself with a mustache, wearing a black hat and trench coat.

My mother tucked her in at last. "Cheer up dear. Tomorrow is Thanksgiving. You may even get a present." She smiled and closed the door.

Now that was news to me. Never before had we received presents at Thanksgiving (then we'd never had a goose before either). Sure enough, the next morning there was a box of crayons and a brand new animal colouring book at her breakfast spot. Later, as I was helping Suzie colour inside the lines, I noticed that one page had been removed from the book. No need to wonder what that page had depicted.

Then I helped Suzie make posters, all the time remembering what happened to spies and gamblers when they were found out.

After awhile, things seemed to settle down a little. It was Thanksgiving – a real holiday. We went out with neighbours to get a pumpkin for Halloween. Actually, we got three. A big one for the front window and two smaller ones for Suzie and me. We drew up plans to see who could make the scariest face. It was fun.

Finally it was time for dinner. It had been smelling good for several hours. Mother was a most excellent cook. There was apple cider and soda pop, potatoes, peas, carrots, cauliflower, but not broccoli, three coloured jellied salads with marshmallows and apple and pumpkin pies. And the crown jewel–the main course.

At last they took the hot, steaming fragrant roasting pan from the oven. The aroma flooded the kitchen. Our mouths began to water.

There were no vegetarians in our family. Unlike past years, father did the carving on the counter far away from the table. Everyone was excited and hungry from the day out. It seemed we had put yesterday's horror behind us. Father dug into the meal with gusto – holidays and festive meals were rare in our house. Besides, it wasn't that dry old turkey.

Everything was going swimmingly well, until, caught up in the ecstasy of the meal, father dropped the "G" word. Psychologists and psychiatrists tell us that words can be both powerful and hurtful things. Besides, no matter how hard you try to swallow them, once they're out there, they're out there forever.

"What did you say? What did you say?" Suzie screamed and then weeping as never before, she rushed from the table.

So ended our festive holiday. As I looked down at my plate, I was pretty sure we wouldn't be having leftovers this year.

Youth is a spontaneous and irrepressible time. Every day promises new adventures and there is no moment greater than the present. Children can mend and move on more quickly than adults. After many hushed conversations and a multitude of apologies, sprinkled with unexpected gifts, things almost returned to normal. Somehow I convinced Suzie that I was only trying to help. Gradually I lost my double agent stigma. We were pals again.

About two weeks later, mother made an announcement at dinner.

"Listen children, your father is very, very sorry about Thanksgiving and he has something to say."

Even though it had been two full weeks, no one was ready to use the "G" word. It was the proverbial elephant in the room, except that it wasn't an elephant. Gerald had become the Thanksgiving incident. Because mother had surrendered the floor to father, I knew we were in for some really big news. Father pushed back his shoulders, clasped his hands tightly and fixed us with unwavering, if misty, eyes.

"Look kids, I am really sorry about Thanksgiving. It was an awful mistake. A terrible misunderstanding and I apologize. Now if you are very good between now and December, I will get you a puppy for Christmas."

Suzie's eyes went saucer-wide and then spilled over with tears. Flowing waterworks and wracking sobs began. She grabbed me by the neck and burbled into my ear. Mother and father looked on in anguished wonderment.

In frustration father blurted out, "What the devil is the matter now? I said I was sorry! What is she saying? Why is she crying, for Pete's sake?"

I hugged her to me. As sometimes happens in families, now it was the children against the parents.

Looking my dad in the eye, I responded, "She just said, if she won't eat goose, why do you think she would eat a dog?"

Chapter II

School Days, School Days

A scary cloakroom, a class bully and learning the joys and dangers of riding double and playing baseball were among the highlights of my elementary school education.

◆　　　◆　　　◆

My First Day at School

Who doesn't remember their first day of school? I will never forget mine. It was full of anticipation, excitement and misery. What made it memorable was that I had to live through it. *Twice.* It became miserable because of my cherished blazer.

My school was about a 20 minute walk from our home and, of course, I walked. As far as I know *everyone* walked. I'm not sure that school buses had been invented back in the 1940's. I know *I* never saw one. All I saw was a bunch of kids walking to and from school. Because it was the first day of school, mother was going to walk with me.

She said it was important to look nice the first day, and she had laid out my clothes on the dresser the night before. There were new shoes, new socks and a new blue shirt. Blue was my favorite colour. Of course there was new underwear. In those days mothers were very keen on new underwear. My mother always said make sure you have clean underwear in case you get in an accident. As for me, I just didn't want an accident *in* my underwear. Anyway the whole outfit looked good except for one thing.

"Ah mom, not the short pants", I complained. "I don't want to wear them. None of the other guys will be wearing short pants."

Mother looked up from the clothes and said, "According to the radio, it's going to be hot and very humid. Close to 90 degrees. By lunch time you'll be glad you're wearing shorts. Very practical for a day like today."

Mother was always practical. She said it was important to be practical. People who weren't practical could end up dreaming their lives away. Even at the age of six I knew that mother was only half right. It might turn out to be 90 degrees, but I'd never be happy wearing shorts. But I had an idea.

So I asked, "Okay mom, if I wear the shorts, can I wear my blazer?"

As far as *I was concerned*, my blazer was my best piece of clothing–not counting my baseball glove and ice skates of course. It was a trim coat with shiny gold buttons. There were tiny anchors on the buttons, but you had to look close to see them. The blazer looked just like the one my father wore in the navy.

Mother was still being practical. "Now look here young man, if it's too hot for long pants, it's certainly too hot for a wool blazer."

"Come on mom!" I pleaded. "I'll trade the blazer for the shorts. If it gets too hot, I'll just take it off. Come on mom, be a sport."

She smiled, "Well you make sure you take good care of it. Your father bought it special for you. Don't get it all sweaty."

And so it was that we set off for Victoria Public School S.S. #3. I strode along like a true military man-blue shirt, grey shorts and navy blue blazer. Victoria Public School was a hulking three storey brick slab of a building. It towered over the surrounding bungalows. It was surrounded by a tall, chain link fence, outfitted with two huge, sliding gates - complete with padlocks. Scary and spooky, it didn't look like a friendly place for little kids. Students always remember school either as a charming castle or a gruesome dungeon. Over the years, Victoria proved to be an enchanted place, but on that first day, it possessed a dungeon-like quality.

Like all schools of the time, it had two entrances with the words *GIRLS* and *BOYS* carved over the gaping doorways. It was important to keep the sexes separate, even in grade one. Educators wanted to teach us early about the dangers of inter-mingling the sexes. For the next eight years we formed two straight lines before the dual entrances. As for me, I discovered the danger of mixing on my very first day.

Mother and I joined the line outside the classroom. We were met by a tall, handsome woman whose shiny brown hair was enclosed in a neat hair net. Looking like everyone's favorite grandmother, she smiled and greeted us.

"Good morning! My name is Mrs. Brand, welcome to Victoria Public School. If you tell me your name, I'll show you where to sit."

Mrs. Brand had been busy planning for us, and had assigned seats to all the children. Girls on the right side, boys on the left side of the room. It was pretty certain there would be no inter- mingling in our class. The mothers left and we took our seats. Mrs. Brand began to explain our daily routine. There would be reading, spelling, printing and art in the morning. In the afternoon it would be counting, arithmetic and rhythm band. There was a sandbox at one side for people finished first and two goldfish in the bowl that we took turns feeding. She said that we would follow the same routine every day so as to avoid confusion. The first day was a half day so we would have a very short time for each subject.

We hadn't got very far along with "Dick and Jane" when Mrs. Brand walked to my desk. Towering above me she said, "John, you must be very hot in that blazer. I see that Mary has one as well and some of the girls have sweaters. Let's take a short break and I'll explain about the cloakroom. We'll start with the boys and the girls can keep on with their books. John, you follow me. You can be the leader."

And that was my introduction to the dreaded cloakroom. To this day, I don't know why she called it a cloakroom. None of us kids wore cloaks, and neither did Mrs. Brand. In fact, in all the time I was there, I only saw one person wear a cloak. That was the principal, and she only wore it on Halloween. The cloakroom covered the entire back wall. There were two sliding doors at each end, one for the boys and one for the girls.

Mrs. Brand slid the left hand door open and ushered me inside. The room was paneled in brown/black wood and the only light came from the open door behind me. As my eyes adjusted to the dark, I could make out two rows of hooks stretching the length of the wall and shelves protruding at the floor. It was dark and scary, and I was squashed into the middle of the blackness as the other boys crushed in behind me. This was a coffin for Grade One's. A place where a small child could disappear forever. If they closed you in by mistake, I wondered how long it would be before your body was found. As the boys pushed in, they blocked out the only speck of light remaining.

I was glad when Mrs. Brand started talking again.

"This is the cloakroom. The bottom shelf is for your boots and the second one for your lunches," she explained. "You hang your coats on the bottom hook and hats on the upper one. This is for coats, boots and lunches. It is not a playroom so there is to be no fooling around in here. John, you hang your coat on this hook, and everyone stay right where you are. I'm going to bring the girls in the other side."

In the dim light, I took off my blazer and fumbled to find the lower hook. The upper hook was so high it looked like a hanging spot for bad kids. The room was narrow and as dark as a coal mine. Mrs. Brand was right, *it wasn't a playroom.* Not unless you played ghosts, goblins, cemeteries and coffins (which I didn't). It was darker than Ali Baba's cave and not nearly as friendly. The other boys had gone quiet and I could tell they were nervous too. Small prisoners, we waited in the hushed silence of the grave. A trickle of sweat made it down my back.

Now I had to admit that mother was right. If I had left my blazer at home, I wouldn't be crushed in the middle of this black hole with thirteen other smelly boys breathing down my neck. Suddenly the door at the other end opened and a beam of light crept into the children's cupboard.

Mrs. Brand led the girls in and said, "Okay Mary, go down to the middle and hang your blazer beside John's".

Mary shuffled her way towards me. She didn't want to be in there either. I smiled and pointed to the hook. I wasn't sure if she could see my smile, but she did find the hook. Mrs. Brand explained the system of hooks and benches as the girls crowded in, shutting out even more of the light. In grade six we learned about the Black Hole of Calcutta and whenever I heard that phrase or story, the dark cloakroom filled my mind.

Mrs. Brand's voice interrupted my black thoughts. "Okay girls, you follow me and we'll go back to our seats. Boys, you stay where you are until I come back for you. Remember, no fooling around."

She led the girls out and closed the door. With the girls, out went the little light. We all stood quietly, waiting for her return and our deliverance. It seemed to take forever. She was coming back, wasn't she?

"Okay boys, you can come out now," she said. "John, you come out last and please close the door behind you. Come along boys, back to your seats."

I tried to stay close to the boy in front but, in my haste, I tripped over the lower bench. Now all the boys were back in the classroom, I was on my hands and knees in the dark. Commando-style, I inched forward. Focused on the light, I looked neither left nor right. For sure I wasn't going to look behind me.

"Keep going, keep going," I said to myself.

At the entrance I scrambled to my feet, and with a mighty push, closed the sliding door and shut the blackness in. Sweating like a Popsicle in July, I took my seat. Safe again.

The half day dragged on. I was wrapped in my own black misery as Mrs. Brand showed us the rhythm band instruments, the sandbox, the pet turtle and the goldfish. I had only one thought. The cloakroom, the cloakroom—always the cloakroom. How would I get my blazer back at the end of the day? How could I avoid the cloakroom in the days to come? How long could I walk to school without a coat or jacket? Could I fit my lunch inside my desk? *But most of all,* how would I get my blazer back today?

At last, the bell rang and our day was over. After the children filed out, I asked Mrs. Brand if she could open the sliding door. I hoped that she might stand close by, or even go in with me.

She said "Of course, John. I'll help you and the girls with their things. I'll open the door and let you in and then go to the other side with the girls."

My plan wasn't working. Once again, I was going to be all alone in the black hole while she went off with the girls. I made a plan. I would be in and out as quickly as Flash Gordon.

"Okay John, in you go while I look after the girls," she smiled and turned back to the classroom.

I bolted down the dark corridor, grabbed the blazer, and beat a rapid retreat. With a hurried 'thank you' I was out the door and down the hall. Back outside I was free from the cloak room, at least until tomorrow. Or so I thought.

My mother was right. It was very hot so I carried my blazer home. She was working in the kitchen when I arrived.

She smiled, "Hello dear. How was your first day at school?"

Many decades have passed since then. Now I realize that it's difficult, sometimes impossible, to describe the trials and tribulations of the first day. Today we call it the challenge of the learning curve. Others label it an 'initial adjustment'. For me, it was summed up as the cloak room.

I didn't know how to answer so I said, "Fine. It was alright I guess."

Nodding she said, "I bet it was far too hot for the blazer wasn't it? Let me hang it up so it doesn't get too wrinkled."

I handed it to her and she fluffed out the arms. She shook out the wrinkles and then, with a puzzled look, she asked, "John, who is Mary Robinson?"

I looked up and said "I dunno mum. There are two Mary's but I don't know their last names."

"Well, you've got her blazer here. You're going to have to go back to school and get yours."

And so it was that I got to see Victoria Public School, Mrs. Brand and the dreaded cloak room twice in one day.

◆   ◆   ◆

Max and Me

"Hey four eyes. Slow down and wait...or I'll break your leg."

I didn't have to turn around to know who was calling me. It was Max, the new kid in our grade two class. Max had arrived a week before, transferred from another school. Rumour was that he had been kicked out because he beat somebody up. The story had been started by Max. He said that he was named after some German boxer and that was why he liked to fight. He claimed that it was "in his blood" and he "enjoyed spreading blood around."

Max was short and round like a fire hydrant. He was a little on the pudgy side, but no one in our class was about to call him fatso. His melon round face was marked with a black wart on the end of his pig nose. When he flashed his hideous smile, there was a gap between his front teeth. I didn't know Max and he sure wasn't a friend, but, I knew it was best to wait for him. As I slowed, I felt a fat hand grab my shoulder. I looked up and stared into that gap-toothed grin.

The yellow teeth disappeared and he growled, "That's better four eyes. I didn't really want to break your leg. Not today any way. Ha, ha, ha."

There were many awful things about Max, but one of the worst was his sneery laugh. It was a punishing laugh without any friendliness or fun to it. A laugh that froze your blood. A witch's laugh left over from Halloween–that promised bad things to come. Sometimes I would hear the laugh coming from the back of Mrs. Kellogg's grade two classroom. From the very first day, Mrs. Kellogg had sat him in a back seat.

She had arranged the rows like a train. Starting with the engine, dining car, passenger car, freight box car and ending with the caboose. I was in the passenger car, hoping to make it to the dining car or maybe even the engine. Of course, Max was in the caboose and you could tell that he didn't care a lick. In fact, he said he liked the caboose because he could keep his eye on the "creeps" in the front. That spot made it easy for him to pick out people he labeled as "special friends". I knew as his fingers tightened on my shoulder that Max had picked me.

He grinned again, "Say four eyes, I see we live on the same street. I thought maybe we could walk home together and have a little fun on the way. Ha, ha, ha."

So that's the how it began. Max started walking home with me and telling me stories of the mayhem he had inflicted on his previous, so-called "friends". Max seemed to be an equal opportunity tormentor, and I felt certain that it was only a matter of time before I became the latest chapter in his book of victims.

There is an old joke about the kid who loved going to school. What he liked best was the going and coming home, he just didn't care for the part in between. Before Max came along, I had enjoyed everything about school. Now I hated going home. My fear built throughout the day and, by lunch time, I was beginning to worry about the walk home. I began to hope that he would miss school. Unfortunately he was very healthy. Max had led me through the gates of hell and I knew I had to tell someone.

"Hello dear, how was school today?" Mother looked up from the counter as she grated some carrots.

Without meeting her eyes, I mumbled, "It was alright, I guess."

She stopped grating and asked, "Well, you don't look alright. So, what's the matter?"

Now was my chance. I took a deep breath and blurted, "It's about this guy, Max."

"Is that the fat little friend who walks home with you every day?" she asked.

I could feel my eyes beginning to fill. "Max, he's not a friend. He keeps picking on me and threatening to beat me up. What should I do?"

She put down the grater and gave me a long look, "Has he ever hit you?"

With a groan, I said "No, he hasn't done anything like that. He just keeps saying crazy things and threatening to do stuff."

After a moment she said, "Well, if he hasn't hit you, that's a good thing. Just stay away from him. You could avoid him by coming home the back way."

As kids, we are really lucky to have mothers, for a variety of reasons. They help us in a lot of different ways. Sometimes they come up with really good ideas. We had two lots behind our house where father tended his garden. I could come home by the back street and then cut through the garden into our backyard. It was a great idea! I could feel dark clouds disappear as I made plans to avoid Max. Maybe if I did it long enough, he would find someone else to pick on. That would be good for me...but not for someone else. I put my plans into action and enjoyed several happy days.

At the beginning of the second week my paradise was shattered by a familiar voice. "Hey, four eyes, where have you been? Don't you want to walk home with me anymore? Ha, ha, ha."

Max was back. There was no escape. We began taking the usual route home. He seemed to be meaner than ever and I noticed that he had a purple mark under his eye. I asked Bobby G. if Max had gotten into a fight. Bobby said "No", that he had heard that Max' father had gotten mad at him because he was getting into so much trouble. I didn't really care. From where I was standing, the black eye looked good on him. But it did seem to make him angrier.

Grabbing my arm, he said, "Listen up four eyes. Don't try hiding on me or I'll have to hurt you bad. I might just knock your head off and put it in a box."

We were into the old routine, Max and me and the long walk home. A walk full of bragging stories, warnings and threats. Sometimes he put his hand on my shoulder and squeezed hard. It wasn't a punch or a hit, more like a warning of things to come. I felt trapped and scared. Mother said I should ask father because he would know what to do.

We had just finished supper and father looked up and said, "So, I hear you're having trouble with some kid. Is that right?"

Now I had a second chance. The words tumbled out as I told of Max's arrival at school, his fights, his detentions, but most of all, him threatening me and our long walks home. I seemed to go on forever. The more I talked, the more worked up I got. At last, I got tired, ran out of gas and stopped.

Father gave me a hard look and said, "Well, if I was home in time, I could speak to Max and tell him to stop." For a second, the clouds broke again and I started a weak, short-lived smile. "But, that won't work. I don't get home in time and it wouldn't really help anyway. Sooner or later you're going to have to find a way to stand up to Max."

I can't say that I really liked plan number two. I had no idea how I would ever put a stop to Max. I looked at Suzie who was finishing her Jell-O. I thought how lucky she was. She didn't have to go to school until next year. If she was really lucky, she might never meet Max.

The long walks home continued as autumn turned to winter. Max said he liked winter because "blood always looked brighter in the snow". Max had a weird fascination with blood - his own and that of other's. Of course, he much preferred to see other people's. I was miserable as Christmas, usually my favorite time, approached. It was the last week before the Christmas holiday and Max was jabbering away about how "friends were supposed to share presents—or else!" Getting rid of Max would have been the best present ever, but I could see no hope of that.

As we neared my house I could see Suzie standing at the end of the driveway. She was dying to go to school and would often wait outside to meet me. That day, she was pushing a bit of snow from the sidewalk with her little shovel.

Max said, "Hey four eyes, there's your little sister waiting for you again." I gave Suzie a weak smile and a small wave. Max turned from her and growled at me, "Four eyes, did you tell your sister how I was going to tear your head off and put it in a box. Ha, ha…"

Max didn't get out the last "Ha" because Suzie brought her shovel down on the back of his head. As Max straightened up, I grabbed the shovel and hit him in the knee. Then Suzie and I ran for the backyard. When we got into the house, we could hear mother at the front door. A tearful Max was complaining that we had hit him with the shovel for no reason.

Mother was grim-faced and angry. "Well young man, let that be a lesson to you. Quit picking on my son. If I were you, I would walk on the other side of the street from now on."

For the next few days, Suzie waited at the end of the driveway with what she called her "head-in-a-box" shovel. She didn't really have to because Max was now walking on the other side of the street. Max and his father moved again before the end of the school year. But, thanks to Suzie, he had been out of my life long before that.

◆   ◆   ◆

A Bicycle Built for Two

"Come on Trott, get aboard. We got a game. Say, when are you going to get your own bike?"

As I clambered up onto Bucky's handlebar, I knew that was the $64 question. When was I going to get a bike of my own? I was almost ten and probably the oldest male on our street without a bicycle. Of course there might have been a few girls who didn't have one, but at that age we usually didn't count girls. When was I going to get a bike of my own?

When you're a kid, a bicycle is more than just transportation; it's your ticket to freedom. Of course you can use it to travel to and from baseball games and practices, but it's for other stuff too. My gang used their bikes to get out to bus stop 26, where you could go swimming in the tip of Lake St. Clair before it ran into the polluted Detroit River. You could get over the tracks and out of the sticks. You could cruise the green avenue of Riverside and see how the other half lived. In the other direction, you could head away from the sprawling city and explore the fast disappearing woods and farmlands. If I ever did get a bike I'd get out and pedal around the streets as the sun came up and my neighbourhood came awake. It would be a quiet, simple and solitary pleasure.

"Hey Trott, climb on and let's get going before we're late for the game."

That had been the first time I had ridden with him, and it had been almost a year ago.

"Okay, where do you want me?" I asked.

"Put your butt on the centre piece, keep your legs out and hold onto the inside of the handlebars."

I climbed up and reached behind to grab a piece of the handlebars.

"Is this safe?"

Bucky snorted. "It's fine. I can see around you and I got good balance. It's fine."

"I meant is it safe for me?"

Another snort and then, "As long as you hold on and stay balanced in the middle, you'll be alright."

"What if I slip or you hit a bump and I fall off?"

"Then you're road kill I guess."

Two years older, Bucky had a quiet authority, a weird sense of humour and absolutely no diplomacy. He had owned a bike for so long that some younger kids thought he had been born on it. It was a real beauty.

His father worked in Detroit and it was a Schwinn bike with fat, white, balloon tires and wider, white fenders. He had stuffed red, white and blue ribbons out of the tiny holes at the ends of the handle grips. Naturally, there were playing cards clipped to the spokes, and a couple of years before, he had attached two flags – a red Ensign and the American stars and stripes - to the back sprockets. Barreling down the street with ribbons flowing, flags flying and cards clacking, Bucky was beyond cool. He had the Cadillac of bicycles, and we all knew it.

I had been asking for a bike since right after Grade One. That was the year the twins got bikes for going into Grade Two. Father said that their father had more money than brains and they were spoiled brats. They may have been spoiled but their bicycles were pretty sharp. I told Father that going to school involved a lot of sacrifices – you ate a packed lunch, you stayed all day and put in your time, you didn't get out until almost four o'clock and then you came home after a hard day's work. He said I could add one more thing to my list and that would be walking to and from school.

In the following three years, the number of cyclists in my gang threatened to become a traffic jam. There was real excitement when Alfred the English Kid showed up with a Raleigh three speed. At first we didn't know what a three speed meant, but Alfred proved that it was faster and easier to pedal. Bucky just snorted and said it depended whether you wanted to ride a Cadillac or a skinny sports car. Bobby G. got a secondhand bike from his uncle and fixed it up. One day, little David and his sister showed up with matching two wheelers. Soon I found myself the only kid on the block without a bike and riding on Bucky's handlebars.

If I didn't have a bike it wasn't for lack of trying. Every year, I put on a big Christmas blitz. I left the Eaton's and Simpson's catalogues lying around open to the bicycle page. I cut out pictures from magazines and old catalogues and left them in strategic places – beside the ash tray and on the back of the toilet. Once I found a special coloured picture of a small boy with a big smile standing beside a shiny red C.C.M. bicycle. The picture was so good that I thought it was sure fire. I taped it to the mirror of my parents' bedroom dresser. I never saw the picture again and the tape disappeared from its normal place.

Father's answer was always the same. "Maybe next year when things are a little better. Right now, times are kind of unsettled. Besides you're a little too short. Next year you'll be taller."

His argument might have made sense when I was in Grade One, but now it was his standard reply. Although I was doing my best on the growing business, I wasn't making much progress. When Mrs. Johnson told us that girls mature quicker than boys and that some boys don't really start growing until they're thirteen, I figured I was doomed. If I was going to ride a bike to school, it might turn out to be high school.

I decided to try a more long term campaign with mother. Shortly after Halloween, I placed a picture of a boy with a bike at her breakfast place every Monday morning. I figured that would give her the whole week to consider the matter. To the picture I attached a valuable contribution which my bike could make to the family. I could get to and from school more quickly which would give me more time for household chores. In cases of emergency, like accidents or illness, I could ride for help. I could pick up food and stuff from Bremmer's market. With a bike, I could get a paper route and bring in big bucks for the family. I was in the process of developing a long list when mother said that she got the point, and I should give it a rest for a while. In spite of my best efforts, Christmas never did bring a bicycle.

I continued to ride to the ball games with Bucky and although I missed out on other trips, I was satisfied. The system might have gone on longer if mother hadn't decided to have tea with Mrs. Cook on her front veranda. I had made a point of getting off two blocks from home because I was pretty sure my parents wouldn't approve of my dual ridership program. I never expected mother to walk three blocks for an old cup of tea. Mother caught me by surprise when I got home, but her comment was even more surprising.

"Well young man, what in the world were you doing riding on Bucky's handlebars?"

"Aaah, I was just hitching a ride home from the ball game. No big deal."

"No big deal! You could have fallen and gotten hurt. Do you think I raised you this long so you could become road kill?"

Road kill? Where did she come up with that expression? I never heard her say anything like that before. For a minute I thought that she must have been talking to Bucky, but that wasn't likely. The long and the short of it was that I had to promise that there would be no more handlebar riding. I was in a fix and out of ideas. Lucky for me, I got a case of the flu.

I was pretty sick and had to stay in bed for three days. It was a boring time, but I could hear the kitchen radio from my bedroom. In those days radio had a variety of programs not just canned music. Most of them were soap operas designed to entertain women as they went about their daily chores. They weren't that interesting and probably speeded my recovery. But there was one that sparked my interest and got me thinking.

Queen for a Day was a very popular contestant program at the time. The show was hosted by a friendly man. He interviewed two or three women who had lots of problems. Some were ill or had sick children; others had suffered fires, floods or tornadoes; and many had lost their husbands somehow. Sometimes the women would start to cry and there would be commercials to sell soap and household cleaner. Then the best story, and the winner, would be crowned Queen for a Day. The other women got a year's supply of soap and household cleaner. I don't know if any of them got husbands back or whether they even wanted them. The Queen got cash, prizes and, sometimes, a trip

The show got me thinking and so I asked mother, "How can I get on that radio show? I want to ask the man for some gifts just like the women get."

"Oh, you can't get on that program. It's called Queen for a day, and it's only for women."

"Well, that doesn't seem fair. Maybe they should have a show for kids. They could call them princes or princesses or something."

She smiled, "This is about getting a bicycle, isn't it?"

I nodded.

"Well, you'll get a bike some day. You just have to be patient and wait for things to settle down a bit."

I wasn't convinced. I wrote to the man and suggested that he start a program for kids. I even said if that was too much trouble, I would settle for a bicycle. I was trying to be fair and help out. I went back to school and didn't hear the show again. But I wondered about those women and their lost husbands for a long time.

"Come on Trott, get aboard." It was Bucky and the start of another season.

"Hey man, I can't go."

"What do you mean, you can't go. You always go with me."

"My parents said I can't ride on your handlebars, it's too dangerous."

Bucky nodded. "Oh yeah, I forgot. No handlebars, right! Well, get on the seat and I'll peddle standing up."

"Well I don't know. They said no double riding."

"No they didn't, they said no handlebars. It's a nice safe seat. Now let's get going."

It didn't sound right, but Bucky could be convincing. Besides, I wanted to go, and it felt safer, even if I did have to look at the dirt in the creases of his neck. My parents always said "no news was good news" and as I climbed aboard, I was determined not to give them any news.

We had played a couple of games when father asked me about the season.

"So John, how's the baseball going?"

"Good, real good. We had some good practices and won our first two games."

He smiled. "That's swell. And you're getting there on time?"

That's when the red flag, the danger flag, the red danger flag went up. If I said anything I would be asking for trouble, so I just nodded.

"Well, I just wondered because Ernie Racine said he saw you riding double behind that Thompson kid again. You know how your mother feels about that, so I want it to stop. Okay?"

So that was the end of that. I was pretty miserable even though my birthday was coming up. I knew I wouldn't get a bike because birthdays were for small, useful presents like socks and underwear. No, the best thing about birthdays was the birthday dinner. Mother said that everyone could order whatever they wanted on their birthday. Suzie always had spare ribs, mashed potatoes, vegetable and strawberry shortcake for dessert. I asked for fried chicken, French fries, corn bread and double chocolate cake because there were no strawberries in May. Just thinking about the dinner made me feel a little better.

At breakfast everyone sang "Happy Birthday," and then father said, "I know it's your birthday, but will you pick up the milk off the back porch so mother can make batter for the chicken."

I stepped outside and reached for the milk bottle. There it was, standing on the back stoop just like always–only this time it was standing behind a shiny red C.C.M. I forgot the milk and bolted back inside.

"Holy cow, holy cow! Thanks a lot. This is great! Is it for me?"

Father smiled, "Well your mother and I don't want it and it's your birthday. I guess it's yours. Besides we don't want you to get hurt riding double."

I was beyond excited. I grabbed Suzie from the table and we both rushed outside.

"Look at the bike Suzie. Isn't it great?"

She looked at it bug eyed but her smile faded fast.

"What's the matter? Don't you like it?"

He eyes began to fill. "It's really, really nice but I want one, too."

Without thinking, I blurted, "Oh, you're too small for a bike." Then I remembered how I felt when people had said that to me. "I can teach you to ride mine and then maybe they'll get you one."

"Do you really think that they'd get me a bike?"

I thought for a moment, and then I said, "After you've learned to ride, I'll let you ride double and then you'll get one for sure. As long as you hold on and don't become road kill."

◆   ◆   ◆

Disorganized Play

"Get your stuff, grab your bike and we'll meet at school. Let's play some ball!"

As a youngster I attended Victoria Public School S.S. # 3 on the outskirts of Windsor, the school no longer exists but after WW II it served as a centre for our recreational as well as our educational development. At school our gang tended to excel in recess. After the school day ended and the gates were locked, the six foot high chain length fence guarded our personal playing field. There were no "Private Property" "No Trespassing" signs which are so prevalent today. Not that such signs would have interfered with our quest for sports. Within the confines of the fence, we locked the rest of the world out, and enjoyed many hours of disorganized play. With the exception of the Bobby G. incident, there were never any problems.

Even though we didn't have coaches, umpires or sports cards, we regarded ourselves as a team. A pick up, play-out bunch of East Enders. If we weren't exactly dead end kids, we operated out of a pretty tight cul-de-sac.

Bucky was a year or two older than the rest of us and an unelected leader. He was the first to bend and shape the Navy surplus gob hats which we wore and the first to attach playing cards to the spokes of his bicycle. One fourth of July he showed up with two handle bar flags–a red Ensign and an American stars and stripes. They were very neat, but we all knew it was better not to ask how he had acquired them.

David was the youngest of the bunch, an overweight runt with a perpetual runny nose. In more popular times he might not have made the team, but we preceded the baby boom and warm bodies were at a premium. David would have been classified as a bench player, but of course there were no benches where we played. He was cooperative, eager to please and would play anywhere. We made him the catcher. His bulk made up for his lack of ability, and if he couldn't catch it, he could at least block it. He might have been a goalie but he couldn't skate either. Most of the time he was more of a back stop than a catcher.

Terry was probably the best athlete of the bunch and would grow into a strong and strapping man. In grade six he was a tall and skinny kid with good hand-eye coordination and a lot of natural speed. "Let me tell you", he boasted, "back at my old school, I once caught a ball before it was hit."

"Sure you did," interrupted Peter (a.k.a. the Lip), "who was the batter, you're mother, I bet?"

Peter was our short stop and resident baseball expert. He believed he was the illegitimate son of Leo Durocher and played like him. He kept up a constant chatter that was an annoyance to both team mates and opponents. He said that he was so good on ground balls that we should call him the vacuum. Over the years, we called him a lot of the things but vacuum wasn't one of them.

Our biggest challenge was Alfred. Alfred the English kid. His parents had arrived right after the war and Alfred had a peculiar accent. When he showed up at the first practice with a cricket bat, we knew there was work to be done. Because he didn't know the first thing about baseball we put him at first base, and told him to catch the ball and keep his foot on the bag. After two years, Alfred became Al, lost most of his accent and acquired several new expressions (none of which were suitable for mixed company).

At third was big, strong Henry who threw the ball so hard to first that it caused Al to flinch at times. He hated to be called Henry and gave himself the nickname Hercules. Given his size, strength and natural aggression none of us raised any objections. Sometimes we let him pitch but he had a tendency to hit certain batters (not always by accident). Hercules Hank was a bulldog but sometimes we had to keep him on a short leash.

Bobby G. was my best friend. A guy who could keep a secret, help out in a pinch, and as we would soon learn—a team mate who never complained. Because we were always short players, Bobby and I shared the field. I would have been described as good field no bat. Together we almost got the job done.

So that was the team, more or less. Because it was pick up, catch as catch can activity, our numbers varied. It wasn't always easy to find an opponent and when we couldn't, we split up for twenty-one or a game of scrub-one. It didn't really matter; the point was that we were always playing at baseball.

Five years later there was a population boom. Contractors built houses, people moved in and organized soft ball came to the neighbourhood. The whole gang became members of the Canada Tavern Rockets. We sported purple and orange shirts complete with beer ads. We had made it to the majors and we were a pretty proud bunch. There were organized practices and scheduled games but we knew that we had become a team on the playing fields at Victoria Public. And every single guy could have told you the very day it happened.

On the Saturday in question we gathered bats, balls, mounted our bikes and headed for the school yard. As usual, the gate was locked and there was no one around. The chain link fence stood tall, strong and welcoming as ever. We threw the bats and balls over, and scaled the fence like commandoes in a WW II movie. At least that's how it looked to us.

This wasn't a mere scrimmage, but a real game with a bunch of guys from the other side of the tracks. As they arrived, you could tell that they were no rag-tag bunch. They carried themselves like royalty—princes of the diamond. They were pretty surprised when we told them that they had to climb the fence.

A tall, red-headed kid looked at us across the fence like we were maximum security inmates and said to no one in particular, "Hey, which one of you rubes is going to come around and unlock the gate?"

For a moment fire flashed in Bucky's eyes and then sweet as a single to left, he said, "No can do! I'm afraid it's up and over for you boys. Unless of course, you want to stay on that side and forfeit the game?"

Quick as a hard, fast chin duster, big red responded with a sneer. 'Where we come from, there's a caretaker to unlock the gate and clean up the field.'

Sounding like Ty Cobb on a bad day, Bucky shot back, "Well, there ain't a caretaker here, so you'll have to get your butts over if you want to play." By now, I was pretty sure that this wasn't going to be a friendly match.

Grinning, the red head answered, "No problem. If we throw our equipment bags over, have you got anybody there that can catch them?"

The bags shot over the fence like stones from Roman catapults and we knew it was important to make good, clean catches. Once they were over, Bucky pointed to the side line to the right side of home plate. As the home team, we took the other side. Quickly they divided into groups of three and began tossing baseballs back and forth. Outside of TV games, I had never seen so many baseballs. Bucky said we should let them provide the game ball, and then if any got lost in the grass, we could find them later. He told Bobby and me not to look too hard for lost game balls.

Al noticed it first and said, "Look they're all wearing white t-shirts and blue stretch pants." "It's almost like a uniform for Pete's sake!"

Ever feisty, Bucky didn't seem impressed. "Well, let's make sure those shirts aren't white for too long."

Then, Peter the Lip chimed in, "Just remember, Leo always says they put their pants on just like us—one leg at a time."

Looking them over, Terry said, "I don't know about that. But they all got them on frontwards and they sure look like they know what they're doing with the baseballs."

Their warm ups had taken them further and further from each other and the throws were strong and accurate. By now, we were transfixed—staring at them as if they were the first Martian team to play a home and home on earth!

Awe struck, Little David exclaimed, "Look every one of them has his own glove. Maybe we could borrow one when we go to the field?"

Bucky sensed that our confidence was leaking like air out of a blown tire. It was time to take charge. "We ain't borrowing nobody's glove. David you got a glove, so stop your whining. Most of you in-fielders are okay and John and Bobby never use gloves out in the pasture. We'll be fine. Let's shake hands and play a little baseball."

Quick as a fastball, the Riverside boys stowed their gear and brought out their bats. Bucky headed to the pitcher's mound and crouching behind the plate, little David looked up at the first batter with a timid grin. You could tell he wasn't concerned about winning, he just hoped to get out of the game alive. Bobby and I jogged to our position in the outfield; as usual we were missing a centre fielder so we shifted around to cover as much territory as possible. Bucky kicked dirt around the mound, Al pounded his fist into his first baseman's glove and Peter the Lip began jabbering. The game was on.

Bucky pitched well and at the top of the fifth, the Riverside Boys had a 4-2 lead. Bobby and I continued to share the outfield, with me in right and Bobby in left. Although we shifted a little, centre field was up for grabs. There were a couple of guys on base when their big guy came up to bat. Bobby and I adjusted a little, moved back and hoped it would be enough. There was a solid crack and as soon as the ball left the bat I knew I couldn't get to it. It would be a double for sure.

Bobby must have been wearing DiMaggio shoes that day because even though it was beyond his reach, he tracked it well. At the last second he reached high over his shoulder and managed to get his hand on the ball. After it was all over, he said he took a bite out of the ball, but we all laughed and said that the ball got the bigger bite. He did get a hand on it, but it was not the complete and entire hand. It was not at the proper angle either, which is why his finger split open.

I was the first to reach him and hollered, "Cheeze Bobby, I've never seen anything like that!" The bone is really white! Cheeze, does it hurt?"

Bobby looked down in shock and said, "Nope. Doesn't hurt at all. Not a bit.'

Soon we were surrounded by the others who wanted a good look. Everyone, including Bobby, stared at the split flesh and white bone in amazement. He held the finger for all to see as if he was exhibiting a captured toad or an unusual bird. By now the Riverside Boys had joined us and we all gazed, thunderstruck, and frozen in time.

Bucky broke the silence, "Okay, okay. Let's get organized. Somebody give me a hankie to wrap this thing up."

Big red looked to Bucky and said, "Our guys will give you a hand. Tell us what you want us to do."

Throughout all our games and practices, the gang never displayed greater teamwork than in getting Bobby over the fence and back home. We boosted Little David to the top of the fence from which he executed his usual, awkward sprawling fall. On the other side, he mounted his bike and rode home for help. Bucky organized us into a rough semblance of the human pyramid we had seen at the circus. With the two teams we were able to create a pyramid on each side of the fence and got Bobby and his finger safely to the other side.

And so it was that we organized our own games, found our own fields, supplied our own equipment–and in Bobby's case–took care of our own injured. With our bikes we were able to roam freely, do what we wanted, and play a little baseball on our own terms. We liked it that way.

◆　　　◆　　　◆

Chapter III

Father Knows Best?

Once my nervous father finally got his driver's license, the rest of the family discovered that his anxiety attacks were contagious.

◆　　　◆　　　◆

Father's Driving Lessons

Learning to drive can be a traumatic experience. Certainly it's a nervous time not only for the student but also for family, friends, neighbours and, sometimes, unsuspecting pedestrians. It's been said that if someone wants to learn to drive you shouldn't stand in their way. In my father's case, it wasn't advisable to stand behind him either! Dad took his first driving lessons when he was about thirty-five (with one or two gray hairs). He was still in his mid-thirties when he finally got his license. But, the amount of gray had increased for those around him.

Experts contend that it's best to learn to drive while you are young. You are less inhibited; your reflexes are quicker; and highway traffic laws are more lenient for minors. Besides, as a teenager you know everything anyway, and you're not using your own car.

It was through no fault of his own that my father came to driving later in life. He grew up on a farm when horses, not trucks, or tractors, were the prime mode of power. He handled these animals at an early age, but found that the skills with regard to mechanical horsepower were *not* transferable. During the Depression he spent most of his time walking, hitching or riding the rails as he traveled province to province in search of work. At that time, cars were for *other* people.

Many veterans acquired new skills and practical knowledge during World War II. Some of my uncles were in the army and spent years driving trucks and jeeps. One was an air force mechanic. My father was in the navy and stationed in Halifax, Nova Scotia. Since there was little need for corvette or destroyer experience in our neighbourhood, when my father returned home, he found himself landlocked. My mother said that joining the navy had been a poor choice (although their uniforms were a lot nicer).

Father claimed that driving was no big deal and that he could learn to drive anytime he wanted. Mother pointed out that since he was a father of two children, and a sole wage earner who lived in the sticks ten miles from the auto plant, *sooner* would be better than *later*. It wasn't that my mother wasn't sympathetic to his plight. She was. She had acquired rudimentary driving knowledge via her brothers and, earlier, from boyfriends. This is not to say that she knew how to drive. She didn't. She had just enough theory to give unsolicited and unwelcome advice to my already nervous father. Needless-to-say, he declined her assistance, on more than one occasion, as I recall.

"Well, if you won't take my help, how are you ever going to learn?" she demanded. As usual, she was ahead of my father in the planning department.

After staring at the spot on the floor as if it were a hieroglyphic eye chart, he looked up and said, "Don't know. Hadn't thought about that."

"Why don't you ask one of your brothers? They have cars."

At that time, my uncles had cars and had driven for years. They had been in the army with the ugly khaki uniforms. As the eldest son, my father had too much pride to take lessons from one of the boys.

Suddenly his face brightened with the glow of the morning sun and, exhibiting a mile-wide smile, he said, "I know. I'll take lessons from my friend Clarence."

With a gasp, my mother choked, "Clarence? Clarence doesn't even own a car!"

"I know, I know, but he drives the garbage truck all day long. It's the same thing."

With that he headed for the telephone.

It was 7:30 in the evening and two days later, when Clarence and the garbage truck rumbled down the street and turned into the driveway. From the sidewalk, my sister and I gaped with mouths open as wide as the trucks loading tray. Grim faced, my mother spread protective arms like wigwags at the railroad crossing.

She exclaimed, "Children, stay back! Get back and be quiet! Your father's going out driving. So be still and don't make him nervous. Driving makes him nervous so be very, very quiet."

We looked at my father who stood ram-rod straight as if awaiting his decommissioning orders. Perhaps he was indeed dreaming of Halifax. It was obvious that my mother's pep talk had done nothing to ease his fears.

My uncle Clarence was a big, genial man who hadn't a care in the world. His critics claimed that he passed all his worries onto others. But, he was happy in his six foot plus skin. He loved his truck, the Black Beauty, and his burgeoning garbage business. As he said, in good times or bad times, there would always be garbage, so he would always have work. It wasn't a career recommended by guidance counselors, but he thrived on it.

"Hi everybody," he beamed. "Pardon the smell but me and old Black Beauty have come right from work. Okay Johnny, are you ready to do a little trucking? Hop in and we'll get rolling. No, no Johnny! You should get behind the wheel if you want to drive."

In a futile attempt to escape, my father had tried to sneak into the passenger seat. Still smiling, Clarence slapped him on the back and escorted him to the other door. With a sheepish grin, my father gave us a mock salute and clambered up. Not an auspicious beginning.

"Okay Johnny. We'll make the first one easy. We'll just practice going back and forth in the driveway. No road tests tonight."

At a time of primitive communication, rotary telephones, party lines, telegrams and door-to-door postal service, it was surprising how quickly the news of a late afternoon garbage delivery sped up and down the street. The neighbours' blinds went up and curtains were pushed aside. Across the street, a man watering his lawn hosed down his wife in an attempt to get a better view.

And that was when a gang of my friends arrived.

"Hey guys, look! Old Man Trott's going to drive the garbage truck. Let's get a good spot."

They spread themselves across the lawn as if that was a safe area.

Survivors often claim that the disaster occurred with unexpected and frightening suddenness. This one fit that bill. Peering to the left and right as if he were entering an intersection, my father threw the truck into reverse and cleared the lawn of all onlookers.

In that instant, Clarence's smile died.

"Stop, Johnny! Stop! Whoa up! Whoa! Take it out of gear. You're good right here. Let's trade places and I'll get it back on the driveway."

Human beings can be an irrepressible lot. In these situations someone will always say, "Well, it could have been worse." In this case they were right.

My friends helped me and my sister get the garbage back into the truck. There was no damage to Black Beauty, and my father claimed that the lawn had been badly in need of reseeding.

Uncle Clarence suggested they should stop for the day and go for chips and beer. He promised to borrow a small car for the next lesson. My mother busied herself splinting up a damaged rose bush. But I heard her mutter that she could have used a beer as much as the next fella. It was pretty quiet around the house after uncle Clarence left. The lessons continued but the big black garbage truck never appeared on our street again.

◆　　　◆　　　◆

Father Takes His Driving Test

The next week Uncle Clarence showed up with a small, family-type car-a Plymouth or a Ford, I think. Not too long and only medium width. This was important because he and father were about to resume the backing out of the driveway lesson. Clarence was dedicated and persistent. He had promised to teach my dad to drive and he was going to do it, even if it killed him.

As for my father, he could not shake the image of Black Beauty idling on the front lawn. My mother was still concerned about her rose bushes, and she offered to help by giving directions from the presumably safe sidewalk. This time father headed right for the driver's seat so I knew he was making progress. He started the car; shifted into gear and began a tentative and erratic reverse.

Cool and calm, Clarence was patience personified.

"Okay, okay Johnny, you overcorrected a bit. Take your time," he instructed. "Come forward, straighten it out and we'll try again."

At the same time, mother, who had retreated to the safety of the flower bed, shouted from the middle of a spirea bush, "Johnny, for goodness sake be careful. You're all over the sidewalk."

From my vantage point I could see that, although the car was on the sidewalk, it was still at least two feet from the front lawn. That was progress. I could also hear Clarence instructing my father.

"Okay, let's try it again. Put it in reverse and back up slowly. Be careful you don't run over Mabel," he cautioned.

Until that moment, I'm sure father had never considered that maneuver. Then again, looking back on all the unsolicited "helpful" hints and caring cautions that mother offered, the temptation may have arisen.

The process continued. Clarence offered his advice. Father moved the car forward and backward, and mother served as a human range-finder from her position on the sidewalk. It proved to be a noisy, if not memorable, practice. I'm sure it was disappointing for the neighbours who had gathered in ghoulish anticipation of another misadventure. Thankfully, sunset came early at that time of year. Since no one was up for night driving, the practice was called on account of "darkness."

After that, driving lessons took place in unknown locations, far away from our house, my mother and the curious neighbours. Uncle Clarence would arrive and my father would slide into the passenger seat and be whisked away. All the nieghbours agreed that Clarence was a most proficient backer-upper, but we could tell they were disappointed. Mother used the time to work on the roses and her other plants. She said that they had suffered such a shock over the last two weeks that she doubted any would bloom.

Modern drivers don't realize how good they have it with turn signals, automatic transmissions, power steering, brakes and windows. Today's automobiles practically drive themselves. That may explain why you see many people eating, drinking, reading maps and talking on cell phones while their vehicles speed through traffic.

Of course, in the early 1950's, father had none of these advantages. In the evening he studied from a large manual provided by the Ministry of Transport. The book was so big it looked like a telephone directory, in training. There were lots of diagrams, a few illustrations and many warnings printed in large block letters. In those days, driving was a serious business. Father pored over the book after work, and of course, mother helped him with it (even though she said there were a few things in there that sounded downright silly). Clarence said the written exam was a piece of cake. It all hinged on the driving test. That was the big hurdle. I'm not sure that made father feel any better.

Clarence did emphasize a few things.

He cautioned, "Now remember Johnny, *always*, and *I do mean always*, signal your turn. Police are death on that. Not signaling will get you a $10 ticket sure as shooting."

Today, some smart-alec would calculate that $10 in the 1950's is the equivalent of $358.32. I'm not sure why they do that, unless they want to make us feel bad and long for a 12 cent loaf of bread. Anyway, ten bucks was big money in those days and a mountain of money for my father. He studied the diagrams of hand signals like Michelangelo examining the ceiling of the Sistine chapel. Arm straight out for left turn, bent at the elbow for the right. I even caught him practicing as he listened to the ball game on the radio.

Clarence advised, "Make sure you roll down the window or you'll really crack your arm. Some day they will have windows that roll down by themselves, but not yet."

I thought Clarence had been watching too much Flash Gordon when he talked about automatic, self-rolling windows. But he was a stickler on turn signals.

The weekly lessons continued throughout the summer and my father's confidence and enthusiasm grew with each outing. Whether this was because of increased proficiency, or the fact that the lessons concluded with a beer or two, I can't say. I know mother said if that's what driving was all about, she was going to take lessons from Uncle Clarence as soon as father finished.

I didn't believe she would ever get a license because she had a nervous temperament. I think she was nervous because she was worried a lot. She was a natural-born worrier. Where somebody else might worry about tomorrow or next week, mother could build worries into next month or next year. In fact, before she passed on at eighty-six, she got to worrying about decades in advance. Given her age, I told her that it seemed a bit unnecessary. She just sniffed and said it never hurt to be prepared. She was a "first class" worrier. And if you were around her long enough, you realized it was a contagious condition. When she finally got her license, after several unsuccessful attempts, *the whole family worried.*

Near the end of the summer, father came home from work, had a shower, gobbled his supper, had two more showers and put on his Sunday church clothes.

Watching the proceedings, mother warned us, "Now you children be quiet and don't do or say anything to make your father nervous. He's going for his driving test and you know how nervous he gets. So don't make him nervous."

Smiling, she turned to my father.

Seeking to reassure him, she said, "Don't worry dear, you'll be okay. You're doing a lot better in the driveway since we moved the bushes. You'll be fine as long as they don't make you parallel park. My brothers say a lot of people fail that one."

I don't think they had ever practiced parallel parking because father gave her a funny look. Clarence said it was time to hit the road and that they might be a little later because they were going out of the city for the test. He had arranged for the test to take place in a little farming community nearby. He knew the driving inspector and said there would be less traffic because the farmers would be tending their cows. Most shops were also closed Wednesday afternoons. Mother said uncle Clarence knew so many angles that he should have been a math teacher.

My sister and I were in our beds when my father returned. He must have got his license because I heard him say he was going to drive them all to the tavern for one celebratory beer and bag of chips. I whispered to Suzie that I was going to take driving lessons soon thinking I could get pop and chips too. She pointed out that they didn't give licenses to ten-year-olds and that I was too nervous anyways. Now that I reflect on it, my sister did possess some of my mother's characteristics. After that, we just listened to the adults.

My mother said she would be happy to go because she wanted to talk to Clarence about driving lessons.

Father said, "Okay, it's settled. Let's go down and get a beer. Clarence, don't feel bad. It could have happened to anybody. It sure taught me a lesson and you were dead right about that signaling business."

It seems that as they were on their way through what Uncle Clarence called "a one horse town," he forgot to signal a turn. Quick as a stop sign, the local constable pulled him over and gave him one of those famous ten dollar tickets. After all his warnings, father thought it was kind of funny, but Uncle Clarence was madder than a scalded chicken. Said he didn't think it was right for police to hide behind bushes like a bunch of highway men. Said it sent a bad message to young people. He also said he thought the cop was just waiting for dark so he could go off to a blind pig somewhere. It was about the longest and loudest speech I ever heard him give. Father said they might have two beers to calm him down and they'd better get going. So, they left, and as far as I know, signaled every turn on the way.

◆   ◆   ◆

Father Buys a Car

My father was a bit of a maverick although, for the most part, he kept it hidden inside. He didn't always take the road most travelled. In fact, sometimes he made his own path through the bush. If he ended up lost, well that was part of the experience. He wouldn't stand in a line for any reason. He said the Depression and the navy cured him of that along with a lot of other things. He treasured a bargain, loved to haggle and regarded "paying the sticker price" as personal humiliation. Making any "major" purchase brought out the rebel in him.

Once father got his license it was expected that he would buy a car immediately. My sister and I expected it. As an employee and resident of the nation's automobile manufacturing centre, his company and his city *expected* it. Of course, no one expected it more than mother.

The wife of a navy man, mother had acquired some nautical strategies over the years. The next weekend she fired her opening salvo.

"Good morning dear. Where is it?" she smiled.

Father shifted his gaze from the cereal bowl and did a quick reconnaissance of the room just as if he was manning a periscope.

Discovering no unusual objects he was forced to ask, "Where is what?"

Now that she had him in her sights, she would not soon disengage. "Where is our car? Now that you have a license, everyone expects you to get a car."

As usual, mother was right. Windsor, Ontario was across the river from the motor city of Detroit, Michigan. Windsor, known as the "wheeled city," was the Canadian counterpart. Auto manufacturing was the primary industry. Cars were a major factor in our lives. They provided employment, shelter, food and clothing. My grandfather, father, uncles and older cousins all worked for automobile factories. Were it not for the fact that after World War II, Rosie the Rivetter had been banished from production lines, it's entirely possible that my mother and aunts would also have worked there. Our family was so tied to the automobile that motor oil, rather than blood, ran through our veins. In short, cars were *everywhere* in our lives. Everywhere except in our driveway and that was mother's point.

Over the years father had been involved in enough of these verbal skirmishes to know that a best defense was a surprise offense. Seizing the initiative, he responded.

"Actually, I thought I'd call Clarence right after breakfast. If he's not busy we might go on a scouting mission today."

Some people are rendered speechless when they find the tables turned; my mother was not one of those shrinking types. In winking good time, she said, "Well, that's fine. You know, if you two need any help I could get a sitter and come along."

Mother was always a great one to help out. Advice and suggestions were her specialties. If she couldn't steer the boat, she wanted to have both oars in the water. Even on defense, she managed to score points.

Momentarily off guard, father floundered, then righted the course and said, "Oh, I don't know. I'll see what Clarence says. Probably not room in the garbage truck for three. Likely won't get a car on the first trip. We'll just tour around, kick some tires and check out the prices. Anyways, I'll see what Clarence says."

Now it was two against one. Mother could see which way the ship was sailing. It would be an all male cruise. "Alright dear, just remember, I'm available if you two boys need any help."

And so she exited the field of conflict with grace and dignity. Father resumed his attack on the cereal.

After breakfast, father got cleaned up and came out dressed in his deal making outfit. Crisp checked shirt, dark blazer, tan pants and highly polished brown shoes. He looked a cross between George Raft and Joseph Cotton. A man not to be trifled with. This was the suit he wore on his periodic farm-buying expeditions. Usually, this ensemble filled mother with dread. Born and raised on a farm which she left one hour after reaching majority, she had no desire to resume agricultural drudgery. However, now that he was on the trail of a car, she gave the wheeler-dealer outfit her full approval.

It is said that clothes make a man and this combination transformed father. It infused him with confidence and increased his contrary personality. When everyone else in the family entered the army, father joined the navy. While all the rest worked at Ford Motor Company, father was a Chrysler man. This was the greatest deviation of all. In the 1950's automobile affiliation was character defining. Employees were expected to be company men in the strongest sense of the word.

Naturally, corporations promoted the connection. There were company picnics, company sports teams, and company excursions. Every fall, before the new models became public, the companies rented large showrooms, cloaked the cars in tarpaulins and invited employees and families to a grand opening and private showing. A real festive occasion. There were balloons for the children and free hot dogs, ice cream, coffee and soft drinks. There were also many helpful salesmen with pens ready. They were armed with detailed information on the latest improvements and blank order books. It was expected that *company men* drove *company cars*. It wasn't exactly treason to consort with the competitors but it was in poor taste. In the conformist 1950's, it wasn't done. People just didn't swim against the stream.

Purchasing a car is a long and involved process especially when it's your first car. Rome wasn't built in a day and chariots weren't acquired in that time span either. Most of father's shopping was confined to the weekends and in those days, everything was closed Sunday. As a result Saturday was negotiating day and Sunday was limited to what he called "tire kicking."

As the weeks turned into months, mother grew impatient.

She resorted to her standard question, "Okay Johnny, where is it?"

Ever the canny shopper, father was not about to be rushed.

He smiled and said, "Well right now, I guess it's still on a lot somewhere."

By the somewhere, my mother was certain that he had yet to decide on a particular car. So she seized on the word. "When is the *somewhere* going to be in the driveway?"

Once in a hunt, father was neither distracted nor hurried. So with a smile, the answer remained the same. "Soon dear, soon."

As a youth of the Depression, father was a shrewd shopper and a canny, savvy bargain hunter. Some might have called him cheap. He regarded himself as frugal. Where some people said that a penny saved was a penny earned, he would squeeze the syrup out of the maple leaf on the coin.

He rarely made big purchases so when he did, he sought pleasure as well as profit. He could engage salesmen in charming conversations so long that their eyes glazed over and their pens ran dry. He could also snap shut like an oyster protecting its pearl. He said he liked to stretch the salesmen even if they didn't enjoy the process. Come hell or high water, the best deal would carry the day.

After ten years even mighty Troy fell, and one Saturday father warned everyone to be home for lunch at noon. Then he went off in his deal making outfit. By 11:45 a.m., we lined ourselves along the driveway eager to pipe the captain ashore. At 12:01 p.m., father, with a smile as wide as a windshield, drove up in a 1948, British racing green Sliver Streak. The car had a sleek torpedo shape with a streamlined and powerful appearance. Now we would call it a "hot car." Today it would be classified as a unique collector's item. Father called it a real bargain.

"Well, what do you think? Isn't it a beauty?" he boasted.

My sister and I began to circle the car with ever increasing speed.

"Wow, it's beautiful!" gushed Suzie.

I added, "Awfully sharp dad, awfully sharp."

Mother stared with dinner plate eyes and her mouth turned down at the corners. "Oh, Johnny, what have you done? What have you done? You didn't buy it?"

Chest swelling he answered, "Lock, stock and barrel. It's all ours, right down to the whitewalls."

Mother gave the car a long, hard look and said, "Well, I just hope you know what you're doing. I guess I should say, what *you've* done."

It was a phrase we had all heard before. Whenever mother told any of us that she hoped we knew what we were doing, it had several layers of meaning. First, it meant that she didn't approve of whatever it was. Second, that we must have been temporarily insane and, more to the point, that she had washed her hands of the entire affair.

Father adopted a bulldog pout and in Churchillian tones responded, "I don't care what anyone says. It was a real bargain and I like it."

He didn't like the car, he *loved* it. For the next two weeks he spent almost as much time washing and waxing as he did driving. Of course, in those far off and older times there was no such thing as car-detailing. Had there been, they wouldn't have got within two car lengths of the Silver Streak. Only father could undertake the washing, drying, waxing and buffing of our car. After a thorough training period, I was allowed to clean the interior, under very close supervision.

"Okay son, I think you're ready to work on the interior. That's the heart of any vessel so let's make sure it's shipshape. Now take off your shoes, climb inside and give her the old spit and polish finish."

I knew spit and polish was just his navy talk; there would be no spitting in his baby. So armed with a whisk broom, soft cloths, wood and window polish, I tackled the interior while father did his magic outside. It was a true labour of love and, with a ballgame on the radio, an all afternoon commitment.

Two weeks after the purchase and four or five wash and wax jobs later, father announced that we were going to having a "coming out" party for the Silver Streak. Mother looked at him with a question.

"What do you mean a 'coming out party'? The car's been in the driveway for two weeks. You ought to build a garage for the poor thing!"

Now father had the plan and he answered, "All in good time, my dear, all in good time. Tomorrow we're driving to the family reunion on Lake Erie. It'll be the first time the boys have seen the new buggy."

Being the eldest, my father always referred to his brothers as "the boys." He also saw himself as the leader of the clan; a trailblazer who marked out new paths and set different standards. That night after school and work we headed out to clean the car yet again.

"Tell your mother that we'll be awhile and ask if she could bring out a bit of supper. I'm going to rig up a light for us in case it gets dark before we're finished."

Like a Carthaginian Messenger heading into a heavily fortified Roman camp, I went inside to deliver the message. We had never eaten outside before and I knew my mother didn't deliver meals to wheels.

She looked at me for a long time and then she said, "Okay, if that's what he wants then sandwiches and nothing except hot coffee. Sometimes I think he left his brain in that car. Maybe we should go back to riding the bus."

I just nodded with a slight grin. I knew she didn't mean a word of it—especially the part about riding the bus.

We finished just before nine o'clock so that we could hear Lamont Cranston and "the Shadow" on the radio. But before that, dad handed me a new tarp.

"Before we go in, give me a hand with this new cover son. We don't want any night birds or wandering cats to spoil our work."

Soon the Silver Streak was clothed in a colour-matching tarpaulin. It had never looked better as it settled in for the night.

The next morning father was the first one up and out. He had put away the tarp and was doing some final buffing when we arrived, loaded down with picnic baskets, beach towels and bathing suits, a sun umbrella and several lounge chairs.

Catching sight of us, father called out, "Just a minute. Hold on! Don't touch a thing! I'll arrange that stuff in the trunk so that it doesn't roll around. Don't touch anything! Let me put these new blankets on the seats so we don't ruin the upholstery. Be careful now! Wipe your feet and don't leave any smudge marks on the handles or the windows."

I think mother said "Humbug" or words to that effect, as she settled into the passenger seat. Underway, the car hummed along. The drive took longer than usual as father avoided short cuts and gravel roads. We stuck to the pavement at a speed guaranteed not to raise any dust.

By the time we got there, the entire clan had arrived and set up their places. Looking back, I realize our timing had been just as carefully planned as any naval engagement. We all exited the car with care, on the lookout for soiled shoes and smudgy hands. As we set up our spot, the boys began to wander over right on cue.

"How are you folks doing?" asked uncle Gordie. "Say, is that a new car?"

My father stretched out his hand and beamed.

"No, a couple of years old. It just looks new."

By now Ernie had arrived.

"Wow, it sure looks sporty. Does it run as good as it looks?"

"Better," said my father with a broad grin. "If it wasn't for the picnic, I'd take you for a spin."

Then the youngest, uncle Don, examined the grill.

"Say, is this some kind of Chrysler? It sure isn't a Ford!"

My father grinned slyly. The trap snapped shut.

"No, it' not. Not a Chrysler, not a Ford. This here is a Pontiac Silver Streak, made by G.M."

"A G.M.!" the Uncles chorused. "Imagine that? A GM. I never thought I'd see the day!"

My father, the maverick, chuckled with satisfaction.

"Well, now you have," he said. "And ain't she a beauty."

◆   ◆   ◆

Mother, Father and John

Like Father

Like son

Suzie Arrives

Having tea in the sticks

Suzie squeals on John

Mother and the Gang

**The family vacation at Rusell's Cabins
Mother, John, Sandy and Suzie**

John, Sylvia (Suzie), Sandy, Guy

Grandson Matthew and Organized Play

Chapter IV

Family Vacations and Holidays

Who is to say that there is no fun in dysfunction? Whether it was Christmas, family reunions or vacations, holidays always brought out the best and the worst in our house.

◆   ◆   ◆

Father Builds a Christmas Tree

Father loved Christmas and usually began preparations well in advance. But one year he decided to change his practice, at least where our Christmas tree was concerned. Many people decorate their tree on Christmas Eve. It's part of a religious or social custom. Sometimes it's just family tradition. One year because of plant layoffs and father's frugality, we did it out of necessity. Father said he wasn't cheap, just cautious with money. As a child of the depression, he always sought a good bargain. Now that I look back on it, he might have had a cheap side to him.

Just because he wasn't going to buy a tree early didn't mean he wouldn't look. He began prowling the nearby tree lots the second week of December. He compared the types available: spruce, cedar, and pine. He lifted them and shook their branches. Were they green and supple or beginning to dry out? Size and shape were also a consideration, but they could be altered if need be. But always, first and foremost, was the price. He refused to involve the rest of the family, but after his solitary inspection, we got a full report.

At supper he said, "You wouldn't believe what they want for trees this year! That chiseler by the gas station wants six dollars and even the Catholic Church is asking five!" He was warming up, "It's outrageous! The church, of all people, is taking advantage of a religious celebration!" Going back to his roots, he added, "When I was a boy we said money didn't grow on trees. Well, I guess it does now. Outrageous, it's just outrageous!"

By the time he finished his monetary tirade, we knew we were still a long way from getting a tree. But he kept right on searching. Every evening after supper he made his patrol of the neighbourhood lots. As the big day drew closer, prices began to drop as did selection.

Now was the time for father to summon up his horse trading skills. During his earlier visits he had remained distant and aloof. He focused on the trees, and rarely spoke to the dealers. When father turned on the charm he made Cary Grant look like an ill-bred rapscallion. And it was charm time. Warm and expansive, he radiated the spirit of the season. He inquired about their business, their families and their plans for the holidays. Almost as an afterthought, he would bring up the question of price. As for the vendors, they were relieved. Previously they had regarded the solitary and skulking visitor as a probable thief. It was reassuring to see him as a potential customer – albeit, a reluctant one.

Of course father brought us up to date on the state of the Christmas tree market at supper.

"Well the lots are thinning out and the price is coming down a bit," he began. "The church is asking three dollars but they don't have many left. The hardware store has dropped to four." He began fuming again, "The chiseller at the gas station still wants five dollars. I hope he gets stuck with a bundle. I know he'll never get my business."

From that we drew two conclusions. First, he didn't like the fellow at the gas station, and second, we wouldn't see a Christmas tree anytime soon. Mother figured that based on Father's track record, he was at least four days away from buying a tree. That would bring us to just one day after Christmas. To be fair, father never did wait until Christmas morning. Of course he might have been prevented by commercial by-laws and government vending licenses. No one would be open Christmas morning. Our tree would have to be a Christmas Eve purchase.

It was a little before 8 PM on Christmas Eve when father came up the walk with our Christmas tree. Actually, he had a small shrub in one hand and bundle of branches in the other.

Mother opened the door and exclaimed, "What on earth do you have there?"

Beaming, father answered, "Why, it's our Christmas tree. At least it will be when I'm finished."

Mother stated the obvious, "It looks like a small bush with a bunch of branches."

Father, the bargain hunter, didn't give an inch. "Wait till it's finished. I really took that chiseller. You know he wanted three dollars for all this! I said a buck and a half, take it or leave it."

Mother looked at the bush and said, "Well, if he gave you the choice, I think you missed a good opportunity. I'm going to finish in the kitchen while you fashion your tree."

Now, in those days, father saved money by cutting the family's hair. He had an old-fashioned pair of hand clippers. They may have been liberated from the navy after the war. The gears were worn, the blades uneven, and sometimes, the handgrips slipped. They pinched and pulled so much that it was impossible to sit still during the process. As a result, a haircut was a long and painful procedure, with erratic and not always flattering results. Father said that the only difference between a good haircut and a bad haircut was a week or ten days. Tonight he had less than 12 hours to create a Christmas tree.

Clearing a spot in the corner, he assembled his tools and equipment. Then, unexpectedly, he called on me and Suzie to assist.

"Now kids gather 'round. Hand me the pieces when I ask for them. We'll work on this together, and make sure you say it's excellent when I'm finished. Okay?"

Suzie and I knew that tomorrow was Christmas; we weren't going to do or say anything that might cost us our presents. We nodded our agreement like the automated reindeer on the house next door.

Father retrieved the stepstool from the kitchen cupboard, and fastened his shrub to the centre of the stool. It was still thin and spindly but it was now taller than me. Securing the ties, he placed it in the corner to hide one of the more obvious bare spots. He took the extra branches from us, and wired them to the front and sides. It began to look a little fuller. In dim light it resembled a misshapen member of the evergreen family. In some ways, it reminded me of one of my haircuts. When he ran out of branches and wire, he stepped back to admire his handiwork.

"Bit short," he mused. "John, hand me the big star that we put on top."

I handed it to him, and he reached down to place it on the tree top. He stepped back again and muttered, "Still a bit on the short side. Pass me the big angel topper that we use for the table."

The angel was really a tall centre piece that he had picked up for a dime at a yard sale. Carefully he placed the angel on top of the star. She didn't look at all comfortable sitting on the pointed end. With a good imagination, one might think she had been Heaven- sent to grace that very spot. Now father could look the angel square in the eye. The truth was, he was a little on the short side.

"Okay kids, let's put on the decorations and remember to hide the bare spots. We have enough do-dads to make this a thing of beauty," he chimed.

Suzie and I brought over the boxes and we all got to work. Suzie was very pleased with the tree because she could almost reach the top. We stopped when father noticed that it was beginning to droop under the weight of the decorations.

Then he said, "Okay, next step. Put on all the tinsel you can find. Let's cover up as much green as we can."

When mother supervised, Suzie and I were never allowed to do so much decorating. We were beginning to like the meager tree. At last we ran out of tinsel, and we all stepped back to view the finished product.

"Well, what do you think?" asked father.

Remembering father's instructions, we both pronounced it excellent. Beaming, father called mother from the kitchen.

She stared into the corner and said, "Well, it won't take up much room, and it doesn't look like it will live too long either."

It didn't. The tree faded fast after the second day. Father was disappointed. He said that like a haircut, it might have improved if it had just hung in for a week or so.

◆   ◆   ◆

Presents in a Christmas Past

Like most, I have fond recollections and pleasant memories of childhood Christmases. I always enjoyed the anticipation that led up to the many surprises Christmas held. Nevertheless, my most memorable Christmas proved to be bittersweet at best.

"So young fella, what do you want for Christmas this year?"

That was the way it began. To this day, the phrase "what do you want for Christmas," conjures up a time when my Christmas magic ended. I was eight and my sister was five in 1950. The year my mother introduced us to the "practicalities" of Christmas and erased the anticipation and mystery of the day. For me, the tinsel on the tree was forever tarnished. It was the first week of December when she made her pronouncement.

"You know, Christmas is coming and it's a very hectic time of year for everyone. I've been thinking that maybe this year you could help your uncles and aunts with your Christmas presents."

Although my mother had never played chess; she was a master of the cunning opening gambit. Whenever she began a conversation with the phrase, "I've been thinking," we all quivered, including father. None of us knew where the conversation was going, but we were pretty certain that we wouldn't like either the *journey* or the *destination*.

The fact that Christmas was coming did not come as a news flash to either my sister or me. In fact, we had started the countdown the day after Halloween. It was not that we were greedy; we just liked gifts and free things. In retrospect, we could have been described as self-centered and acquisitive. Actually, now that I think of it, we were probably just greedy.

For us, Christmas was a lot of things but hectic wasn't one of them. Sure we had to go downtown and visit Santa at Smith's department store, spend hours poring over the Eaton's and Simpson's catalogues and advise our father on the choice of candies and nuts, but that was our job. It was busy but not hectic.

My sister and I were perplexed. We waited open-mouthed for our mother to drop the second Christmas ball. We had learned long ago not to ask her what she meant when she uttered, "I've been thinking." We might have to travel down the road with her, but we weren't going to help start the car.

"I've been thinking that you might help your uncles and aunts by letting them know some of the things you want for Christmas. It would make their shopping *a lot* easier at this hectic time of year," she said with a smile.

There it was that word "hectic" again. Uncertain, we looked at each other, nodded and said it sounded like a good idea. This was a trick our father used whenever mother said "she had been thinking about this, that or the other thing." It worked. My mother went off smiling and humming 'Silent Night'.

Now, in the past, we had left the choice of Christmas presents to our uncles and aunts, and they had done a fine job. There had been many gifts, lots of variety and, most important to me, always a surprise. Sometimes, one or two ran out of time, or ideas, and simply stuffed money in a funny card. My sister and I were magnanimous, and never regarded cold cash as a disappointment or a letdown. From our perspective, their job was to provide the gifts, and our job was to open them. It was that simple.

"What should we do?" my sister asked.

"I don't know. Maybe we could make a list or just tell them what we want," I said.

Even though I had made the suggestion, I was not happy about it. For me the joy of Christmas lay in the suspense–the surprise of opening mysterious packages whose contents were unknown.

In this respect, my sister was a polar opposite. She was a Christmas sleuth. From her very first Christmas, when she crawled up to the tree and ripped the wrapping off six presents–four of which were mine– my sister had to know all about Christmas long before the 25th. My mother called her the Christmas squatter as she sat at the foot of the tree, shaking and turning the presents to and fro. Holding them up to the light, she would try to trace their shapes through the wrapping. So thorough were her inspections, she might have had a great career as a forensic scientist. She became an X-ray technician instead.

To me, the idea of putting in a Christmas order just didn't seem right. It was okay for Santa Claus but not for aunts and uncles. My sister did not share these reservations. She grabbed the Eaton's catalogue and school scribbler, sharpened her pencil, and began her foray into the world of independent market research. With care she copied each key word from the catalogue into her book. As Suzie's list grew longer and longer, my mother warned her against "stockpiling." She said the list was just for one year, but my sister just kept printing.

As for me, there seemed to be no way out of my dilemma. Once I named an actual article the element of surprise would be gone forever. In the next two weeks, aunts and uncles began to drop by, and I watched in anguish as mother introduced the topic of Christmas presents. That was the year I became an adherent to the conspiracy theory of history. Nothing ever transpired by chance. Major events in the world occur because someone, like my mother, just happens to get "an idea."

My sister became a willing participant in what I saw as the plot to wreck Christmas. When asked what she wanted, she would bat her eyes, get close to the person and whisper into their ears. Everyone thought it was so cute, and my sister played the Shirley Temple role to the hilt. Once the guests had left, she rushed to her scribble pad and crossed out another item.

"So young fella, what do you want for Christmas this year?" they asked.

Indecision is no substitute for a real plan. I hadn't the foggiest idea, but now I was under pressure.

In desperation, I blurted, "A hockey stick and puck, a football and maybe a coloured station wagon with a gate that lifts."

I was astonished that this panic-induced confession was accepted with enthusiasm. Even my mother gave an approving smile. It worked so well that it became my standard, scripted answer.

At last the big day–December 25, Christmas–the "day of days" arrived. We dressed, made our beds, and headed down to breakfast. My father, an ex-navy man, said there would be no bed check because it was Christmas. My mother said it had been a hectic time, but her migraine wasn't so bad this year. Like an overworked Christmas elf, I slumped over half a grapefruit and a homemade cinnamon bun. Our traditional Christmas breakfast was as appealing as corrugated cardboard. My sister (a.k.a. Shirley Temple) ate quickly with a spoon in one hand and her scribbler in the other.

Soon we gathered to distribute the presents which my mother had scattered randomly around the tree. Somehow, my sister's presents always seemed to end up clumped together. With notebook and pencil in hand, she began to open her gifts. I noticed that she saved the gift tags and made check marks in her notebook. I was dumbfounded. How could this be the mystery of Christmas? Much later I learned that this was standard operating procedure at baby showers. I guess my sister was just ahead of her time.

My reverie was interrupted by my father, "Come on son, get into the spirit and open a gift!"

I opened my first present and it was a red station wagon with yellow trim and a lifting tail gate. It was almost identical to a later gift–a yellow station wagon with red trim. I opened a strangely wrapped present which proved to be a football.

My sister looked on like a wise, old owl. "I bet you're going to get more! Can't you see that it's the same shape as those other two packages?"

She was right, of course. The three footballs went well with the station wagon fleet and their lifting tail gates. Roch Carrier wrote a story of a French Canadian boy who asks for a hockey sweater and gets a Toronto Maple Leaf jersey instead of the Montreal Canadiens; that kid didn't know how lucky he was. When I finished opening my presents, I had enough hockey sticks and pucks to outfit two forward lines and a couple of defensemen. Everyone could see that the new plan had gone horribly wrong. My Christmas was as wrecked as that old one horse open sleigh.

Ever the realist, my mother pointed out, "Well you did get everything you asked for."

In a futile attempt to console me, my father added, "Cheer up son! You're bound to lose a few pucks and break a stick or two over time."

From behind her mountain of gifts, my sister gave me a smile which was closer to that of the wickedest witch of the west than Shirley Temple. She always was a poor winner.

My mother's face brightened, "Smile, don't look so sad.

Wait till you see what we're having for Christmas dinner. You'll be so happy."

She meant well, but we both knew that the dinner, like the presents around me, had been preplanned. How could the annual roast turkey, mashed potatoes, peas, squash and plum pudding ever be a surprise?

◆   ◆   ◆

Grandfather at the Reunion

Family reunions! Many families have reunions and I'm sure that most of them are very enjoyable. The Trott's had annual reunions, and although most of them were described as unusual or interesting; there was one that was truly memorable. The five star, number one, crème de la crème, was the time that grandfather went missing.

"It is time for the Dominion time check from the capital observatory in Ottawa. There will be ten seconds of silence followed by a long dash. The dash will signal that it is exactly 1:00 PM Eastern Standard Time."

Every afternoon grandfather set his watch according to the CBC time check. A small man, he burrowed into his overstuffed, green arm chair which was positioned beside the tall floor model Philco. Sometimes if he wasn't wearing his plaid shirt, it was difficult to locate him in the folds of the chair. Grandma said that one time he disappeared into the chair for two days. Everyone knew that it was just wishful thinking on her part. The point was that grandfather loved his chair and the CBC news.

"Humph, good to see you. Sit down. I'm not getting up," a typical grandfather greeting. "Radio says Russian's may have the bomb, big fire in Toronto and Chrysler's might go on strike. Supposed to snow in Atikokan and..."

"That's enough Jack. Everybody has radio now. They don't want to hear the news from you." As usual, grandma cut grandfather off. Grandma could be pretty short with grandfather and he wasn't a tall man to begin with.

Grandfather didn't seem to mind. He just retreated into the CBC. He relished recounting the latest reports to guests. He listened to the news every hour on the hour, checking for inaccuracies and the latest updates. The fact that many broadcasts were recorded didn't change a thing; grandfather argued that you never knew when something might happen. The truth was that once he retired from Ford's, not much did. Except for the daily news. Of course, it was impossible to transport the armchair and the Philco, and that may have been one reason that he hated family reunions.

He was not alone in his dislike of the family gatherings. It wasn't that we didn't like to get together and socialize; although most of the time we gave that impression. It was just that our large group dynamics were not good. It might have been genetically generated. We operated better in very small groups—one, or two—maybe three or four at the most. There seemed to be too many unresolved issues, past grievances, unintended slights and too many economic, religious and political differences. Too much small stuff from the past kept popping into the present and warping the future. Everyone was aware of the problems and did their best to avoid conflict—without success.

The identity of the founder of these clam bakes had been lost in the of mists of time. It certainly wasn't grandfather. Had grandma not reminded him, he wouldn't have known about them since they were never announced on the CBC. As for grandma, she denied any involvement in the affair.

"Don't look at me," she said. "I can take'em or leave 'em. Big waste of time and effort as far as I can see. Why do I want to eat cold food and share a blanket in the sand with a lot of screaming kids and pesky ants? Though the strawberry shortcake is good. I just come to be sociable. I can take 'em or leave 'em."

Actually, that was not the total truth. No one could leave them because that would have been an admission of failure. Attendance was compulsory; no mere social request, but rather a matter of familial duty and personal honour. Just as everyone had done their bit for the war effort; now they must pitch in for the reunion. It's true that one aunt had excused herself by packing up and moving to California. But she had always been the risk taker in the tribe. After that her family relationships seemed to improve. Her interaction was limited to sprightly Christmas cards expressing her love and best wishes for the upcoming reunion.

The truth was that a true Trott would have died rather than miss the reunion. In fact two had recently taken that way out. The problem was that the funerals created the same social tensions, and didn't come off well. Aunt Myrtle called everyone out when her husband died.

"Stop your bickering and carrying on. There's no call for this kind of behavior at a funeral. I declare if poor Fred weren't already dead; he'd be totally mortified."

Her comments struck home and everyone realized that death was not an appropriate alternative.

Perhaps we were just too diverse a group. In the late forties there were still a number of working farmers who complained about the weather. Because they practiced different types of agriculture, it was too hot or too cold, too wet or too dry, and the planting was too early or too late. It was apparent that one size of weather would not fit them all. Even God couldn't have pleased everyone. Indeed the deity's existence, nature and influence had been called into question on more than one occasion. The auto workers debated the merits of their competing brands. The women discussed and disagreed on matters such as recipes, cleaning methods and child rearing. Onlookers agreed that Trott's had the most spirited parties in the park. They usually said this as they packed up for an early departure.

Social historians will tell you that communal meals promote social bonding and strengthen relationships. These people never broke bread with the Trott's. In keeping with our character, each group brought their own particular and sometimes peculiar tastes to the table. Natural differences were compounded by sensitivities, allergies and individual eccentricities. The idea of sharing was out of the question as individual families clustered around their own hampers like mice in cheese factories. On one occasion there was the possibility of a breakthrough when everyone agreed that watermelon was the perfect dessert. Alas, agreement was short lived. The next year sixteen watermelons appeared and arguments arose as to the reddest and sweetest, the juiciest. We needed Gertrude Stein to remind as that a watermelon is a watermelon is a watermelon.

Naturally we children followed our parent's example. There was no such thing as a friendly game or cooperative activity. Whether it was foot races, softball,swimming, hide and seek or tug of war, the competition would become fierce. One of our favorite games was a no-holds-bar version of murder ball. We loved it when other kids joined us because we had new targets. The influx of strangers might have united us but for some reason these kids never stayed very long.

Uncle Jack was the self appointed games convener and he loved the job. "Games are good for the body and soul. Good preparation for the school of hard knocks, the hurly burly of life. Now everybody get ready! There are sixteen of you and I have one ball and a dime for the one that brings it back. No sharing." With that he gave the ball a mighty kick, it soared into the stratosphere and the race was on. He once told uncle Fred that the kids couldn't even play solitaire without getting into an argument.

There is no better finish to an outdoor party then a cozy bon fire. Some families gather, sing songs, tell stories and roast marshmallows. It's a good way to wind down, chill out and share heartfelt goodbyes and best wishes. Even this simple pleasure prompted disagreement in the clan. The family was split down the middle as to whether the fire should be set in a log cabin or teepee configuration. The argument was that while one was easier to start; the other burned longer. It was ridiculous but even at the age of ten I found myself committing to the teepee camp. It must have been genetics.

Naturally we also disagreed over the fire starting materials. Should it be newspapers, wood chips or kindling strips? What type of wood was best? Those were the discords and abiding issues which could delay fire lighting long past the younger Trott's bedtime. Everyone did agree that uncle Max's use of gasoline was strictly forbidden. At that point, uncle Max would pursue his blackened lips, raise his singed eyebrows and stomp away.

Of course during the year in question we never got to have a camp fire. It was during a challenge tug-of-war–auto workers versus farmers–that someone noticed that grandfather was missing. After a quick check of the beach and the playground, it was decided that a search party should be organized.

Grandma was having no part of it. "Why, I'd walk a mile barefoot over a bed of coals before I'd traipse after him. Don't worry, he'll be back for supper. Always has been."

It was well known that they didn't always see eye to eye. Some claimed that their union was the genetic source of our conflictual natures. The family genealogists claimed that it went much further back, and that the Trott's had ridden with the brigand William the Conqueror. Four foot, ten inches and two hundred pounds it was hard to imagine grandma walking a mile at the best of times but she did have a way with words and could create striking images. She said she was willing to help out. She volunteered to stay behind and keep eye on the strawberries and such.

Uncle Gord drew a map in the sand and divided the area into search quadrants. Of course there was some discussion about the selection of leaders and the length of the search. Uncle Ernie supplied the kids with sticks and suggested that we beat the bushes if necessary. There were only three search directions since Lake Erie lay to the south. Grandfather couldn't swim, had suffered typhoid as a child and hated water, no sense in searching the lake. We were on the verge of setting out when a small man in a battered fedora, plaid shirt, grey work pants and black boots trudged over the hill. It was grandfather clad in his customary beach wear.

A shout went up from all sides. Like the children rushing to Jesus, the little ones flocked to grandfather. The squad leader uncles strode towards him as if they had something important to say. The women heaved sighs of relief and even grandma looked up from her strawberry shortcake. Grandma believed that you could have your cake and eat it too, if you were quick enough. All and all, it was a welcome worthy of Charles Lindbergh.

Grandfather waved everyone away and made his way to a table in the centre of the picnic area. "Somebody help me up to the table," he ordered. "I've got something to say."

A triumvirate of uncles rushed to his side and every one watched in open mouthed silence. To the best of our knowledge, he had never climbed anything higher than the three steps to his back stoop. For the children watching grandfather clamber on the picnic table was akin to viewing a high wire walker stroll over Niagara Falls. The table was soon ringed with adults; everyone certain that the old man would topple, and hoping that he wouldn't fall in their direction. But grandfather planted himself firmly in the centre, and raised his arms over his head with solemn authority. He was like one of his beloved bantam roosters bringing order to the hen house.

You could tell from his dramatic pause that he listened to the CBC a lot. "I went for a walk and I didn't miss your arguments and disputes. I collected some bottles and cans, and probably made over a dollar." He held up two paper bags for all to see. "If you can't get along, grab a bag and take a walk. Might do you some good."

So that was it. A mini Moses on a picnic table with no ten commandments, just one single message. It got pretty quiet and I suspect some people felt a little ashamed. Everyone knew that he was right. Well, almost everyone. When grandma took the empties back, she said that the whole shooting match only came to seventy-eight cents. When grandfather asked if there was anymore strawberry shortcake, grandma said he was too late; somebody had eaten it all. Grandfather said in that case he would go and wait in the car.

Grandfather is gone now but like many patriarchs, he left a legacy. The picnic table caper was his finest moment. After that, there was a definite change in the reunions. Disagreements were replaced by quiet discussion. Uncle Jack lost his job as games convener. Lunches became cooperative pot lucks. Even the camp fires became fun. Now there were two of them, side by side, and people could wander back and forth from the teepee to the log cabin fire. On the odd occasion, when an argument did break out, we remembered grandfather's advice. Disputants were told to "walk it and bag it." The old man would have been very proud.

◆   ◆   ◆

Father Takes a Vacation

When you're young, people are always asking what you want to be when you grow up. In the late 1940's most kids I knew opted for a fireman, baseball player or cowboy. I belonged to gang of six or seven boys, and we all had these ambitions. I've lost track of them over the years, but as far as I know, none of us achieved our three treasured occupations. Of course, ambitions change with the times. All my father ever wanted to be, was a farmer.

Once he got the Silver Streak, father would take us on Sunday drives after church. Some people drove to the lake, others visited relatives and friends, or toured the city or neighbouring towns. Father never took any of these excursions. He always headed off to the country. We would roll past farm after farm and father would reminisce.

He would point out the window and say, "You see that farm? Belongs to the Frasers. I started working there when I was fourteen."

A little later it would be, "Look it there. There's the Randolphs'. I picked tobacco there three summers in a row."

Still later he would slow down and then say, "That's old man Harvey's place. He grew the best tomatoes in the country. He was a good boss. That was before the depression hit. He lost it all."

At other times he would just drive along commenting on the sights.

That's a mighty fine crop of clover. Too much rain this spring. With water like that in the fields, it's going to be late seeding."

The drives, which most frightened mother, were the ones in which father came armed with the real estate section of the newspaper. These were investigative probes-no reminiscing, no sightseeing-but serious searches. Ground work for these trips usually began the night before. Perusing the newspaper, he would offer to get mother a second cup of coffee.

Then he would ask, "What say we take a special drive after dinner tomorrow?"

With a tightened jaw, mother would respond, "Where did you have in mind?"

Like a trapper laying down a line, he would say, "Well, there's a farm for sale near Ruscam. It's in a good area and I thought I might drive over and take look."

Mother had been born and raised on the farm and left for the big city as soon as she was able. She remembered farm life as long, hard and full of drudgery. The agrarian dream held no allure for her. And so the sparring would begin.

She would answer, "Oh dear, I thought we might visit Tom and Margery. We haven't seen them in so long."

Up until then, none of us had heard of Tom or Margery, so her thought must have been a recent one.

With an advertisement in hand, father was not an easy man to put off. Caught off guard for the moment, he would frown and then smile. You could almost see the light bulb glow in his forehead as he framed his comeback.

"Well, we could see them on our way back. I just wanted to take a look at the farm. We're not going to buy it or anything. It's just to take a look."

The trap snapped shut. And so would begin another long and boring afternoon as father drove, and one farm led to another. Of course these were more than cursory drive-by-viewings. On arrival, it was necessary to talk to the man, examine the house and barns, check out the equipment, and walk the fields.

Ever the gentleman, father would always invite mother to join him.

"Let's get out dear," he would propose. "There's somebody in the yard. We could go over and have chat."

Without looking up, mother's answer was always the same. "You go ahead dear. I'll stay in the car with the kids. I've got my knitting and they can read their comics."

It hadn't taken any of us long to realize that one was never to set out on safaris without a good supply of comics and knitting.

Even worse than the speculative farm tours were the auctions and estate sales. These were all day, pack a lunch, fill a thermos and load several folding chairs affairs. While the rest of us made quick inspections of the junk, father's examination would be as detailed as a Klondike miner seeking the illusive golden vein. He was not about to be rushed. This was one of the few times that mother wished for a longer winter and shorter growing season. Father's dream was to acquire a farm with a little cash and a lot of hope. It never happened. And the weekend farm tours continued throughout my youth.

Father kept his hand in the soil through gardening. When his navy tour was finished, he got a job in the automobile plant, a house in the sticks, and two extra back lots. Near the house he planted fruit trees: apple, pear and plum. He built an arbor for his white, blue and purple grapes. In the flower garden there were a variety of roses and perennials. But it was in the back lot that he unleashed his agricultural passions. There were root crops such as potatoes, beets and carrots. Salad fixings included lettuce, onions and cucumbers. The melons and pumpkins sent their tendrils everywhere. His pride and joy were the tomatoes and the corn. If others planted victory gardens, father's efforts could best be described as unconditional surrender acreage.

It wasn't long before I was enlisted as his assistant. Being small and close to the ground, I became the critter enforcer. In the days before harmful but effective sprays and insecticides, bugs ruled. It was a labour intensive job.

Father demonstrated, "Now son, the trick is to pick 'em up, squeeze their heads and toss them in your bucket. Pick 'em, squeeze 'em, toss 'em. Simple as one two three! Squeeze 'em hard and you'll only have to squeeze 'em once."

Naturally, as a farm labourer, I received a corresponding wage. As I recall, twenty potato bugs were worth a penny. They were cute but prolific. Were it not for my concentrated and diligent efforts, I'm certain that it would have been only a matter of time before, like Lennigen's ants, they would have marched on our house and cut us off from our neighbours. But, next to the corn borers, potato bugs were almost cute and cuddly.

Father cautioned, "Son, keep your eyes open for corn borers. Don't let them inside the leaves or they'll ruin the cob."

Father was right. These pale yellow worms-longer than my thumbnail–could wreak havoc on a corn field. They could also be rather impertinent. Should one strip the leaves and find a corn borer at work, the bug would raise his yellow head, fix you with his dark eyes, as if to say, "I was here first. Go get your own cob."

Corn borers were not pretty but in the ugly contest, they finished a distant second to the tomato worm. Red and green with a smushed-in face and large mandibles, nature had camouflaged them to hide among the tomatoes and vines. Why Mother Nature wanted to protect them was beyond me.

As father said, "They grew up early because they had faces even a mother could not love."

I'm sure that sometime in the 1950's a Hollywood director hit on the idea of using the tomato worm as a model for the hideous predators in the science fiction movies. One glance and you could see that a magnified version could eat New York and all its citizens, without as much as a burp. If consumers knew of the variety and number of insects that thrive on vegetables, there would be a run on dairy products.

Father worked shifts at the factory which meant that some weeks he could tend the garden before going in at 4 p.m. Other times, he would hurry home and get his work in before dark. Whatever the shift, he always found time for the garden. Factory work was hard and could be soul-destroying. Having been through the depression, father said there was no such thing as a bad job. Usually he spent his two week vacation relaxing with his crops. It was a big surprise the year he told the family that we were going away on a real vacation.

With great pride he announced, "Okay everybody, pack your stuff, we're heading north. Heard about this place from a guy at work. A farmer has a few cabins on the back end of the farm. They're right on the lake and it should be pretty nice."

After a long drive, we arrived at our vacation destination.

The Russells lived in an old brick farmhouse. The barns, out-buildings and small pasture were close by. Beyond that, on every side were billowing fields of wheat. Mr. Russell was in his late fifties. A short, squat man who was beginning to bend with age. Years of weather had produced a prune face. His smile remained broad and friendly.

He offered a hearty greeting, "Welcome! You must be Johnny and this is your brood. Did you have any trouble finding the place?"

With a smile father answered, "No, the instructions were good."

"Great. Well, I'm glad you're here. I'll get my truck and you can follow me down to the lake."

He led us down a combined farm lane and logging trail towards Lake Huron. At the bottom of the road was a clearing with three, small wooden cabins. Three hundred feet beyond lay a pebbly-beach and a lake lapping at its edges. We had arrived at 'Russell's Vacation Resort and Rustic Cabins.' Our cabin consisted of one large room with a set of bunk beds anchoring each side. In front of the beds hung a clothesline to which a curtain was attached. The curtain was drawn at night to create a sleeping environment and offer privacy. In the centre of the room was an old farm table with four harvest chairs. The kitchen counter, sink and two-burner hot plate was beneath the window which looked out to the lake. Two frayed arm chairs and a small table stood off in the corner. Simple. Basic. There was no danger that 'Russell's Resort' would be taken over by the Hiltons any time soon.

My sister and I loved the rustic quarters; father thought it was fine and mother said, "It would do."

After settling in, we were given a tour of the outhouse. Then Mr. Russell bowed to mother, shook hands with father and said, "Well, make yourselves at home and enjoy all the amenities. Johnny, I'll see you at seven tomorrow, if that's okay?"

With a smile, father replied, "That will be just fine. I'm looking forward to it."

Soon, we felt right at home. Suzie and I took to the country holiday life like a couple of sheep dogs. There were few, if any, distractions and no other visitors during our stay.

'Russell's Vacation Retreat and Rustic Cabins' were very much a work in progress. But we didn't care. There was more than enough to do. Most of the time mother joined in and a major activity was planned every day. Berry picking, hiking in the woods, rock and shell collecting kept us busy. Every day there was swimming and playing around in an old, dilapidated row boat (which might have been a remnant from the Titanic). One rainy afternoon mother attempted a craft lesson, with mixed results.

Every morning father was first up, made some coffee and toast and then went off to see Mr. Russell. He returned for supper around 6 o'clock. When we asked him to join us during the day, the answer was always the same.

He would smile and say, "Not today. I'm off the see Mr. Russell. Maybe Sunday."

After a while this became a bit of a mystery for Suzie and me.

So I asked, "Hey mom, where does father go every day?"

She replied, "He told you. He goes to see Mr. Russell."

I still didn't understand so I asked again, "Well, what do they do all day?"

She smiled and said, "You know your father. I'm sure they are finding things to keep them busy."

Father never did learn how to swim but before supper he would splash around and get cleaned up. After supper he would sit on the porch in the rickety rocker and smoke a cigarette, awaiting the evening stars. He was relaxed and as calm as the lake after a storm.

When Sunday rolled around we all went berry picking in the woods, had a picnic on the hill and drove into town.

This routine continued for ten days, and then it was time to pack up and head home.

Driving back, we compared notes on our time away. It seemed that everyone had a terrific time. When we asked father what he and Mr. Russell did every day, he said he was helping out. Mother said some people would call it work. Later we found out that father had paid for the holiday by doing farm work for Mr. Russell. We continued to vacation at the Russells' for the next four years. Father the farmer was never happier than when he went on holiday.

Chapter V

Entertainment

Although I was a radio child and avid fan of such dinner time serials as-the Lone Ranger and the Cisco Kid; it was television of the 1950's that transformed my life.

◆　　◆　　◆

The Lone Ranger Anniversary Show

"Okay boys, round'em up, and head'em out. We're off to Abilene."

The late forties and early fifties were the golden age for cowboys. After WW II guys like John Wayne, Ward Bond and Ronald Reagan traded their military uniforms, bazookas and jeeps, for vest and chaps, six guns and horses. Without disappearing into the Pacific Ocean, Hollywood managed to move even further west. Movies, radio, comics and later television, painted thrilling and nostalgic pictures of the old west. Kids loved it and all the little buckaroos my age saddled imaginary horses, toted cap guns and worshipped the cowboy of choice whether it was Roy, Hop-a-Long or the Cisco Kid.

In 1950 if you could scrounge a dime and six Orange Crush bottle caps, you could get into the Saturday matinee at the Tivoli Theatre in Windsor. I had no trouble finding the bottle caps but coming up with the dime was a problem at our house. Over the years, I did go a couple of times with my cousin, Donny, and I got to watch Hollywood's top two cowboys, Roy and Gene, duel it out at the box office. The competition was so intense that it even overflowed into the playground at Victoria Public. My friends Bobby G. and Bucky were leaders of the opposing camps.

Bobby, who was a big Roy Roger's fan, started it all.

"OK so why do they call him the King of the Cowboys, if he's not the best?"

Patterning himself after his hero, Bucky was quick to shoot back, "What do you mean King? Was there an election or something? Roy Rogers dresses like a dude and does more singing than shooting."

"Oh yeah, well Autry's the one that's called the singing cowboy. Besides he's short and fat."

Bucky unloaded a second time, "He's not fat; he's muscular. My dad says he's a working man's cowboy and that Roy's a bit of a queer duck."

Uh oh, a queer duck! That was hitting below the belt and Bobby had to come to the defense of his hero.

"What do you mean, a queer duck? He's married to Dale Evans. Besides, Trigger's a better horse than Champion."

It was becoming a stupid argument, but with those two it could always get worse. Besides, if it was a choice between Dale Evans and Trigger I knew who I'd pick.

"Wrong again. Last week I saw Champion count to twenty in 'Ambush at Sagebrush Flats.'"

I walked away thinking neither of these guys wanted to get into a counting competition with a horse.

We didn't get a television until later on so I got most of my western exposure through the radio, and I didn't feel the least bit short changed. Later on there would be high class adult westerns like Gunsmoke, Tale of the Pioneers and Death Valley Days but they didn't count. I was hooked on the weekly radio shows that played during the supper hour. Although mother and father were not members of the Dr. Spock School of Child Rearing, when it came to supper radio programs, they did show a liberal bent. Cowboys were allowed at supper as long as there was no hooting, hollering or spitting, and of course, cap guns were checked in the bedroom.

Somewhere there's a picture of me sporting Hop-a-Long Cassidy chaps and vest, topped with a black hat. There were pictures of our heroes everywhere in magazines, newspapers and comics. Since imitation is the sincerest form of flattery we copied their styles. I preferred the black hats like Zorro, Lash Larue and Hoppy. You can tell from the picture I'm a tenderfoot but the cap pistol in my left hand and the slight sneer sent a message to posterity that I was not to be trifled with.

The radio corral was full of real and phony cowboys. There were the real, true cowboys like Hop-a-Long, Cisco Kid, Bobby Benson and the B. Bar. B. Riders. Then there were pretenders like Sky King, who as a modern rancher, patrolled the plains in an airplane. Sergeant Preston of the Yukon came across as a wannabe western lawman who had gone north to the Klondike with the miners, gamblers and bushwhackers. Personally I always felt sorry for Preston's horse Rex who played second fiddle to the wonder dog King. No real, true, self-respecting cowboy would ever have let that happen. For hardcore fans, airplanes and dog teams just didn't cut it.

For me there was only one king of the cowboys in radio land. He was larger than life and so mysterious that no company would have thought of manufacturing and selling his costumes. Every kid knew his nickname but no one knew his true identity. For me he blazed a trail that none of the others dared to follow.

"A fiery horse, with the speed of light, a cloud of dust and hearty 'Hi Ho Silver, the Lone Ranger–'Hi Ho Silver,' away! With his faithful Indian companion, Tonto, the daring and resourceful masked rider of the plains, led the fight for law and order in the early west. Return with us now to those, thrilling days of yesteryear. The Lone Ranger rides again..."

There was absolutely no doubt that the Lone Ranger was my hero.

"Mother, did you hear that?" I asked.

"No dear, I was washing the dishes. What did the radio say?"

"Well one month–four weeks from today–they are having a big anniversary show for the Lone Ranger. They're going to tell how he started, the silver bullets, how he met Tonto and why he wears a mask. Isn't that great?"

"It sounds like a lot to put in a half hour radio show. But I know you won't want to miss it."

I was crazy with excitement.

"Oh, you can bet I won't miss it. I'm marking it on the calendar right away. That's going to be the most important Wednesday night of the year."

The Lone Ranger anniversary show was big news back at school. Even the followers of Roy Rogers and Gene Autry listened to the Lone Ranger. On the radio he was number one. Enthusiasm and speculation ran high and everyone had a theory about the anniversary show. Bucky said that the Lone Ranger's parents had been killed in an Indian raid and he had been raised by the tribe as Tonto's half brother. Bobby

G. disagreed. He said that the Lone Ranger and Tonto were escaped prisoners put away by someone like Roy Rogers. They wandered the west in disguise trying to make up for their past crimes. Terry Anderson had seen Death Valley Days on TV. He said that the Lone Ranger's family owned a lost, silver mine. Robbers had killed his whole family and he was searching for revenge. He only went back to the mine when he ran out of silver bullets. It was fun to spin, discuss and alter the stories. But none of it mattered because on the anniversary show we would all learn the truth.

It was six days before the show that Suzie got sick. She had a history of illness. Father said she could pick up a bug faster than Houdini could crack a safe. As I walked through the door, I was hit by a strong, chemical smell. It wasn't mother's floor cleaner—more like something from the medicine cabinet or a hospital.

"What's the stink?" I asked.

"It's camphorated oil, vapour rub and rubbing alcohol. Your sister's sick."

Suzie looked up and gave me a weak smile. Her neck was wrapped in a thick, broad bandage which began at the shoulders and wound its way up to the bottom of her ears. The smell was coming from the bandage, and she didn't look too happy about it.

"Now John, I want you to wash up and make sure you get behind your ears. Put on your good clothes. The three of us are going to see Dr. Digman."

Well, I was sorry about Suzie and all, but this meant a ride on the city bus, and that was a treat. I wondered if I could get the window seat or whether mother would give it to the sickee. There were all sorts of possibilities. In my callous and selfish youth, I just didn't realize how many.

When we got to the doctor's office, mother and Suzie went right in. I got to sit on a hard chair in the waiting room and watch his wife sort through some papers. She was dressed like a nurse but father said she was just his wife. I looked through the magazines but couldn't find any comics. I knew there wouldn't be any—there was never anything in these places for kids. I began to think about all the ways kids got shortchanged. I was just getting into it when I was interrupted by Dr. Digman towering over me.

"Well young man, how are you today? Would you stand up please, so I can take a look at you?"

He was a tall, thin man with dark, horned rimmed glasses, a big nose and a shaving brush moustache. He smelled of tobacco, and I could see a pipe sticking out of his suit pocket. He was so tall that even when I stood up, I felt like I was sitting down.

He bent towards me, and holding out a flat stick he said, "Open your mouth and stick out your tongue son, I want to take a look inside."

I did as I was told because I didn't want to be sick like Suzie. He looked in my mouth, waggled the stick around and turned to mother.

"I don't see anything wrong. But it's probably only a matter of time. I could do them both next week."

Mother smiled and said, "I'll take it up with my husband. It might be best. That way Suzie will have company."

Well, I was told that there was a family conference, but of course, Suzie and I were not there. And then mother broke the news.

"John, Suzie has some bad tonsils and they have to come out. You're both going to the hospital next week for a simple operation."

I wasn't sure where my tonsils were, but my mouth was open so wide that they could have fallen out had they not been attached.

"Why do I have to go just because she has bad tonsils?"

"Well the doctor said it's best to take them out now. That way they won't give you any trouble. Besides, you can keep Suzie company."

At the age of nine, medicine was a mystery to me, and I couldn't understand how taking out my tonsils would make her feel better. As for keeping her company, I did that lots of times and was happy to do it. I liked her a lot. For a girl, she was a real fun person. I kept her company at school, in the backyard, at the beach and playground, and lots of other places, but going with her to the hospital seemed like too much togetherness.

"Ahh, mother," I protested. "Why don't I just go down with her, tuck her in and come home?"

"Listen to me young man; I've already discussed this with the doctor and your father. I'm not going to discuss it with you. You're going with your sister to have your tonsils out and that's final."

In those days, there was a song on the radio that said, "We're on our way to somewhere and we're going to have a happy time."

I don't know why I thought of it then but I did. I was pretty sure that somewhere was the hospital and I was certain that I wasn't going to have a happy time. Lots of people will tell you that their young years were the happiest time of their life. They are usually old people with bad memories who never had their tonsils out; they have forgotten the unfairness of childhood.

"OK, so when is the operation and does it hurt?" I asked.

She smiled. The winners always do.

"There's nothing to worry about. You'll be asleep. You won't feel a thing. You'll be back home the next day and you'll get ice cream after the operation. The doctor will do it Wednesday."

"I can't go on Wednesday."

Her smile vanished like a rabbit in a magician's black hat.

"You have to go. The appointment's been made. Why can't you go?"

"Look at the calendar. That's the Lone Ranger's anniversary show. I can't go."

"Oh dear, I forgot," Mother looked kind of sad.

For an instant I began to smile and then…

"Well, I'm sorry, it can't be helped. Lone Ranger or no Lone Ranger, you're having your tonsils out next Wednesday."

Now there were two rabbits in the black hat and my eyes began to fill.

◆   ◆   ◆

I looked up and saw Dr. Digman staring down at me. Holy smoke! He was wearing a mask too. Only his was white instead of black, and covered his nose and mouth instead of his eyes.

"OK, son, I'm going to put this ether mask over your mouth, breathe in and see if you can count from 100 backwards to 10 in your mind."

I thought, this guy ain't too smart for a doctor. I can do that easy. 100-99-98-97…

"How do you feel now?" mother asked.

She and father were standing beside the bed. I tried to answer but it felt like someone had ripped my throat out. I looked over and saw Suzie sound asleep in the next bed. In the past, she had said she liked hospitals because the sheets felt good, they let you eat in bed and you could sleep as much as you wanted. From where I was lying, it looked like she was having a great time. Even though it was my supper time, I felt sleepy too.

"Look son, I brought a radio. We can listen to the Lone Ranger."

Dad held the radio up, put it on the bed table and plugged it into the wall.

I tried to smile but it hurt too much. I gave him a thumbs up like in the war movies and he signaled back. Maybe this tonsil thing would work out after all. Suzie was having a great time sleeping her head off.

Mother and father were beside us; we might get ice cream and soon we would be joined by the Lone Ranger. The only thing was that I felt pretty tired.

Father switched the radio on and I listened. Soon I heard, "A fiery horse with the speed of light."

I'm not sure but I think I heard "High ho Silver," just before I fell into a deep sleep.

◆　　◆　　◆

T.V. or not T.V.?

T.V. or not T.V.? That was the question. And just like the dilemma in old Elsinore, the issue of television threatened to divide our family in 1952. My uncle was an early advocate while my father was a not so passive resistor. Fortunately, at the end of the day, the only blood spilled and bodies prone were on a small seven inch black and white screen.

"Your brother called and wants us to go over early Friday night for a visit."

My mother's smile would have been that of a happy face logo had they existed in the fabulous fifties.

Scrunching his face like a used dishcloth, my father snorted, "Visit my foot! He just wants to show off his new television. Just another fad. A radio with pictures. I heard he paid an arm and a leg for it. I just hope they don't come to collect the body parts while we're there."

My uncle was sold on T.V. If he wasn't one of the original apostles, he qualified as an early convert. And like every religious zealot, he worshipped daily and sought to proselytize others. For my uncle, living in Windsor in the 1950's was like residing in a combined Mecca/ Jerusalem. Television reception in the city made it the holiest of holies. Across the Detroit River were the three American networks. They were all within reach of the miraculous rabbit ears. Later, Windsor would add its own station and then uncle had access to all four gospels.

Rabbit ears were antennae perched atop early models. Although a few were designed as metal circles, most were two conjoined, flexible, vertical arms attached to a receiving box. Like the old time magician drawing a rabbit from his top hat, these ears plucked the signals from the ether. For my uncle, it was magic of the most amazing kind. For my father, it was radio with pictures.

It is no exaggeration to say that my uncle fell in love with the rabbit's aural appendages. With a single twist, you could strengthen or weaken the signal. This was his magic rod which he loved to wield for family and friends. On clear nights, when the magic was strong, he could amaze one and all by drawing signals form Toledo and Cleveland. It's true that the pictures were fuzzy and the words unintelligible, but everyone agreed there definitely was something out there. With a satisfied smile, he promised that in the future he would get New York City or Boston.

He never did but as the poet said, "a man's reach should exceed his grasp or what's an antenna for?"

Father grumbled, "I don't know why we have to go so early? I'm going to miss the seven o'clock news."

Mother answered in a perky voice, "Well, he has something special to show us. Jean is going to serve dinner while we watch T.V."

When we arrived we were escorted downstairs into a newly paneled room. My sister and I sprawled beside our cousins on the rug while my parents joined my aunt on the chesterfield. A new recliner sat off to the side. My uncle called it the set-up station while my aunt referred to it as the commander's chair. It was empty when we arrived because my uncle was on his knees in a prayerful position before his shrine.

Staring in disbelief, my father asked, "What the devil is he doing? What on earth is that on the screen?"

Aunt Jean said, "Oh, that's a test pattern. It comes on before the shows begin. Gordie loves to adjust it."

We all peered at the strange geometric pattern. It could have been an ancient code or a landing platform for alien flying saucers which were landing with increasing frequency in the early fifties. The test pattern allowed viewers to adjust and sharpen their reception before the regular programming began. My uncle had made his own crystal sets and fiddled with vacuum tubes at an early age. For him, the test pattern adjustments were one of the most interesting aspects of early television. With its air of technological mystery, the test pattern was something that cried out for concentrated attention and diligent adjustment.

From his vantage point, uncle called, "Now watch this everybody."

On his knees before the venerated box, he focused and refocused the pattern. He adjusted the design, sharpened the contrast, controlled the rolling picture, realigned the vertical, and leveled the high pitch whine which was part of the initial set up. For him, volume controls were mere child's play. It was obvious that this nightly ritual involved the whole family. Everyone called out encouragement and advice. It was a constant chorus.

"That's better."

"No, not there."

"A little more to the right; a little more."

"No, it was better before."

"Okay, that's good now. It's good. Stop! Don't move."

The family instructions were so detailed and precise that I would not have been surprised had the entire set taken flight, carrying my uncle with it. At last, my uncle was content.

With a smile bigger than the screen, he called out, "Okay everybody, sit back and relax. It's show time!"

We watched for about three hours: a quiz show, two soap operas and a movie. Halfway through the evening, uncle got up and changed the station. Everyone held their breath as the fiddling resumed. We could tell that was the part that he enjoyed the most. At 10 o'clock, father said that he had about all the fun he could handle for one night and we headed home. On the drive back my parents discussed the evening.

Mother began, "Well, did you have a good visit dear?"

Father snorted, "Visit? We hardly spoke. All we did was watch that cursed idiot box. Why were we sitting in the basement?"

Mother seemed shocked and said, "Why, that's their new T.V. room. He did all the paneling himself."

Father was building a head of steam and answered, "Well, it's still the basement. The man's imprisoned in his own cellar. Thieves could come in and clean out the whole place while he's down there fiddling with that machine. And what did we have for supper?"

Mother said, "Why, Jean made them special. They're called T.V. dinners. They cook fast so you don't miss any of the programs and you can eat them on little trays in front of the T.V."

Father grunted, "They tasted like cardboard. It will be a frosty Friday in July before I go back there."

Safe to say, our initial foray into television was less than a complete success. We were back where we started on the battlements of Denmark with the age old question: T.V. or not T.V.?

◆   ◆   ◆

Television Comes to Our House

Well, it wasn't a frosty Friday but a Saturday night several months later when father said he was going out to play poker. Mother was shocked but not speechless.

"Play poker?" she asked. "You never play poker! You haven't played poker in your whole life."

Up to the challenge, father saw her and raised her two.

"Sure I have," he responded. "We played poker all the time in the Navy. Besides, it's a party for one of the guys at the plant. I said I'd go."

Father didn't get home until quite late and he didn't look real chipper as we got ready for church the next morning. Mother said something about a fool and his money. Father said it wasn't that much and they should drop the subject. So, they did. It was just after the poker that father said he was going to Dobson's Hardware on Friday night to rent a T.V. for the weekend.

In the marketing Hall of Fame there must be a whole section devoted to the concept of weekend T.V. rentals. Now-a-days, with debit and credit cards and new cheaper technology, most people can buy a television anytime they wish. In fact, you can pick one up at the grocery store. I don't know anyone who doesn't have a T.V., and most have more than one. Some even have the complete package: the entertainment centre. It was very different in the '50's. Televisions were complicated, labour intensive and expensive. Their high cost led to the development of the layaway plan and installment buying-a revelation in consumer spending.

For those who had financial or moral reservations about the high cost of televisions, retailers developed the foolproof weekend rental plan. The concept was cheap, simple and almost 100 percent successful. For a modest fee, a family could rent the television from Friday evening until Monday morning. Set up instructions, rabbit ear antenna and a channel list were provided. If you rented for two or more weeks in a row, the rental fee could be deducted from the sale price. The key to success lay in its utter simplicity. The unsuspecting renter took the television home for one, two or three weekends in a row. After that, all he had to do was pry it from the hands of the family members, return it to the store, and have everyone swear off television forever. It simply could not be done.

Suzie and I could not believe our ears. At long last, television was coming to our house! Mother, on the other hand, appeared to be in a state of shock.

She had to ask, "Did you say you were going to pick up a T.V.?"

Father's answer was at the ready.

"Yes, I did dear. I thought it would be nice for the children on the weekend. Now kids, it's not *our* T.V. We're just renting it. It goes back first thing Monday morning. Okay?"

Of course it was okay. Monday was days away and, in between, we would have our very own television. On Friday night, father came home with a Marconi set. It was a long, rectangular, brown box with a five inch viewing screen. The space for tubes, filaments and wires was twenty times larger than the screen. Screen size didn't matter because everyone scrunched around the box as if we were operating a wireless.

In some ways, early television featured the complexity of telegraphy. The pictures had a tendency to roll or develop vertical cross patterns. As a result, the vertical and horizontal controls were critical, and the man of the house had to be ready for instantaneous and repeated adjustments. In Windsor, we picked up three Detroit television channels. Like all those pioneering new territory, the stations were in a learning process. It was common to have programs interrupted with written instructions:

Do Not Adjust Your Set
Experiencing Temporary Problems
Technical Difficulties. Please Stand By

Sometimes there was no warning and the program was wiped out beneath an avalanche of snow. Of course we were used to snow and didn't mind at all. In short, the experience was wonderful and we loved every second.

That night we watched the man in the suit read the news. I had seen him many times in the hardware store window. I began to wonder if he ever got to go home or was he always there reading news, news and more news? After we saw a puppet show; a circus; and a movie about a kid who lost his pony and then found it again. Mother made popcorn and said it was better than the movies because the bathroom wasn't so far away.

Suzie and I were up early on Saturday morning and we watched a test pattern. It wasn't as interesting as the man reading news but it was real T.V. When the stations came on, we watched some primitive black and white, stick-figure cartoons and some old RKO serial westerns that had escaped rather than been released from Hollywood.

In the afternoon, mother joined us at to watch a woman on the cooking show. Mother said the picture was good but the woman didn't know the first thing about cooking. She also expressed concern about the number of pots and pans the woman had dirtied. As for father, he spent the day outside working in the garden and washing the Silver Streak.

During supper, father asked us how we liked the television. Suzie was bubbling over.

"Oh father, it's wonderful. We saw cartoons, cowboys, puppets, singing apples and geometry pictures. I wish we could keep it forever."

For some reason, the kid really liked the test pattern and the singing apples in the Mott's applesauce commercial.

I chimed in, "Yeah, it's great dad. There's lots of good stuff to watch. It might even help us with our school work."

I didn't really believe the last part but I thought that it might help to swing the decision if the vote was close. Mother said that she had been far too busy to watch much but what she had seen was fine.

Father smiled, "Well, that's good. We'll have to try again after supper. Maybe around 7:00 p.m. Who knows what we'll find?"

Everyone hurried through the chores and gathered around the set a few minutes before seven. The man in the suit was just finishing the news again. At that time, we got three Detroit stations and father seemed to know right where to look. He turned the channel from the news and a different man in a sport coat filled the screen.

"Good evening hockey fans. This is Bud Lynch coming to you live from Detroit's Olympia Stadium. Tonight our Detroit Red Wings take on the Toronto Maple Leafs from Canada. So sit back and get ready for three periods of rousing hockey from these perennial rivals."

Father pulled himself closer to the set and said, in mock surprise, "Well look at that, Mabel. It's a live hockey game. We're watching it as it's played. This thing is really amazing."

That night mother watched as hockey came into her home via the T.V. It was an experience she was going to repeat many times, on many networks, over the next fifty years. During that time, she called the never ending sports programs many things but "amazing" was never one of them. After the hockey, Suzie and I went to bed while mother and father stayed up to watch a movie. In the morning mother said that the movie had been very good. She had almost forgotten the hockey game.

After church and Sunday dinner, we gathered around the television once more. There were travel programs, variety shows, and lots of old movies. It seemed that the television provided Hollywood with a great opportunity to clean house. We didn't see the news man in the suit so maybe he got the day off.

All too soon it was time to pack up the set so father could return it Monday morning.

During the process father asked, "Well, what do you think? Should we rent the television again next weekend?"

Now mother seemed to have switched sides.

"I thought you didn't like T.V. You said it was a waste of time and money."

We had all heard him say that so, for now, father had to take the higher road.

He asked us, "Now, now I was thinking of you and the children. Kids, did you enjoy the T.V.?"

That was like asking us whether we enjoyed pancakes, summer holidays or Christmas. Of course we enjoyed T.V.

Suzie got in first, "Oh father, it was great. I really liked the puppets and the singing apples."

"What about you son?" he asked, turning to me.

"Dad it was terrific! My friend Ralph says they have cowboy movies every Saturday morning. The hockey was good too."

I learned early that in life, as in hockey, it helped to stay onside.

Father had three votes but he wanted a unanimous decision. So he pressed mother. "See dear, the kids really loved it. You liked the movies, didn't you?"

Mother enjoyed her role in the opposition but on this issue she swung over reluctantly. "They were very interesting. I didn't say I didn't like it. I just thought you were against it. If you all want it, then go ahead. It's not like we're buying, it's just a weekend rental."

And so the one-eyed monster returned to our house. It was amazing how quickly a pattern developed. Friday night was movies with popcorn. We gathered around the small, flickering box like a Neolithic clan viewing fire for the first time. We had entered a different world. We were hooked. Saturday morning there were more cartoons and cowboys, and in the afternoon, the cooking shows. Always there were the singing apples and the man reading the news.

On Saturday night father said he was surprised that hockey was on again. At least that's what he said. Mother asked if they had watched hockey at the poker game. When father didn't answer, she said she had some ironing to do in the kitchen.

Sunday also went pretty much as the first time except for the dinner.

After dinner father said, "Well, this seems to be working out pretty well". And then he asked, "So what do we do next?"

Mother was on her guard again. "What do you mean what *do we do next*? What *do we do*, about *what*?"

Father was more than ready.

"Should I take the T.V. back and tell him we're through or do we take the next step and buy it?"

Suzie began moaning softly. I was almost hoping that she would turn on the waterworks. But her moaning was pretty effective. It could be decision time so I thought it best just to listen and learn.

Mother's answer was quick. "I thought you said they were a lot of money. In fact, your exact words were 'an outrageous expense.'"

Mother never seemed to forget anything you had once said. She was especially good at remembering careless remarks and hasty outbursts.

"Well, it is a lot of money," father admitted. "But you don't have to pay it all right away. I can put something down now and after six monthly payments, we own it."

Mother wavered, "Well, it was nice and I know the children enjoyed it. I guess we could, if you think it's okay?"

Father beamed and said, "I did some figuring last night and we can handle this. If we don't buy any big item for awhile, it will work out fine."

And so it was that my father, "a child of the depression; a cash on the barrel guy; neither a borrower nor a lender advocate," joined the dollar down and a dollar a week consumerism of the 1950's.

Today it's a truism to say that television transformed our lives and values in radical ways but in 1952, we were just starting down the road. In spite of himself, father brought television to our house. Television brought hockey, baseball and boxing. A year later it even brought a reclining chair for father.

◆   ◆   ◆

Chapter VI

The Battle of the Sexes-Starring Mother and Father

Sometimes my parents found themselves on opposite sides of the fence; luckily for all concerned it proved to be a small and flimsy partition. Farm auctions, yard sales, the birth of a baby, and the world of work all proved to be sources of tension. My brother Guy, who is mentioned in "A Baby for New Year's", was born in 1956, outside of the scope of these stories, and for the most part remains anonymous.

◆　　　◆　　　◆

Father Goes to the Auction

It was early on a Saturday morning in June when mother asked, "So what are your plans for today? Not another auction I hope!"

Father loved auctions. You would have thought for a child of the depression, auctions would have been rife with bad memories. But this was not the case. In fact, it was farm auctions - complete with household furnishings piled on the lawn, tables, chairs, rockers on the front porch, implements and utensils leaning on the fence and farm equipment up and down the laneway-that got his blood percolating.

Mother was not nearly as enthusiastic. In fact, she referred to the sale items as "other peoples' junk." Moreover, she did not subscribe to the old adage that one man's refuse is another's treasure. On the contrary, she believed that one man's junk was another man's garbage-junk was junk! She went on the trips just to make sure that he didn't buy it all: lock, stock and barrel.

Pursing her lips, she would say, "You don't know the man. If I left him on his own, he'd come back with everything *including* the barn. In fact, he'd likely buy the farm!"

Father would smile and say he had no intention of buying the farm. He pointed out that in the forces, the expression "he bought the farm" meant that the person had died.

In his own defense, he added, "I might get a little excited now and then, but I don't intend to have a heart attack over the stuff. I thought we'd run over to a little sale in Colchester. It's a fine day for a family excursion. You can't beat an auction for a good outing."

Because mother accompanied father, it meant that Suzie and I were subjected to what became known as "family jaunts." Separated from our friends and activities, we never found the trips very interesting. I'm not sure what farm kids did for entertainment; but whatever it was, it didn't seem to involve toys. Sale items rarely included anything of interest to children. What toys there were seemed to be well used, in disrepair or completely destroyed. Broken tea sets, cracked bats and unraveling baseballs, ripped playing cards and scuffed checker boards minus several checkers. After a few trips I came to the conclusion that farm kids must be a rough, dour and cheerless bunch. Aside from a few old dogs lazing on the porch and skittish cats with runny eyes, there was little of interest for Suzie and me. As a result, we spent most of our times watching father in action.

He had a simple strategy: arrive early and leave late. Early meant that you could check that everything was in working order and nothing was being squirreled away for the auctioneer's family and friends. It was a time to scout bargains and earmark potential treasures. Although there weren't as many professional dealers as today, father scanned for them, like a hawk on a field mouse. One had to stay late because that's when the *real* bargains appeared. By four or five, the crowd had dwindled and even the auctioneer wanted to get home for supper. In the late afternoon father was at his keenest and mother had an even firmer hold on her leash. For Suzie and me, auction excursions were more than a full day; sometimes they seemed like a complete week.

In the beginning, father was an eclectic shopper. He was open to anything as long as it was in good working order and cheap. Of course, he had a soft spot for old farm items. These were remembrances of his youth. Butter churns, cranks for Model A's, coal oil lamps and lanterns, cultivators, post hole diggers, washboards, buckles from horse collars, hinges, locks and oversize keys, all proved to be items of interest.

"Look at that!" he exclaimed. "We used to have one of those on the farm."

"Well, what is it?" mother asked.

"I'm not sure," Dad admitted. "But it's a real beauty. Let's see how high the bidding goes."

Father's purchases were limited by the state of his pocketbook and the space in the Silver Streak. It was amazing what could be bought for five dollars in the early 1950's. As for the Silver Streak, Suzie and I often rode home sitting atop, or wedged between the "Trott treasures."

Sometimes the quantity of stuff was such that even the most skilled auctioneer had neither the time nor the desire to do the sorting and arrange a display. And so was born the "mystery box." It didn't matter whether the boxes were open or closed, most items were non-identifiable. Father was a sucker for "the mysteries" which went for a dime or a quarter. Naturally, these boxes sat on our laps because there might have been something fragile inside.

After a year or so, his searches took a different turn.

"Did you see this article on the auction?" Father asked.

Mother looked up from her knitting, with less than mild interest, and responded, "You know I don't read that section. Auctions are your department. What did it say?"

Eyes sparkling with excitement, "Seems a fellow bought an old painting for fifty cents and sold it six months later for five hundred dollars," he answered. "Just imagine that?"

Up to that point, father had never thought of the auction as a way to make money. They were outings for fun, "family excursions," but now they had the potential to become money-making ventures. With this new objective, his auction quests became even more intense.

Landscape painting has been a focus for Canadian artists, professional and amateurs, for many, many decades. The auctions were full of old, rock/tree and water pictures. Over the next three years father acquired many. Had they not been in glassed frames, we could have wallpapered with his findings. Soon he had enough that he could rotate this collection with the seasons. The maple trees might be green leafed, autumn blazing or drab and bare; the rivers roaring torrents, dry creek beds or snow encrusted and frozen; and the rocks remained rocks.

According to Canadian history, the struggling Group of Seven never stopped in Essex County for a late supper and sleepover. There is no record of destitute artists paying accommodating farmers with their works of art. Despite his searches, father never found a masterpiece.

He claimed that the glass and frames were worth more than the two dollars he had paid. Unfortunately there seemed to be little market for glass and picture frames at that time.

Our gallery outgrew the house and garage; mother became frosty and father, discouraged. He might have given up auctions entirely had he not come across another newspaper article.

◆   ◆   ◆

Mother Discovers the Yard Sale

Father opened the conversation, "You'll never guess what I heard at the auction last Saturday."

"No, you're right," mother humphed. "I won't even try."

"Well, it seems that a woman bought a box of books for fifty cents and found over a hundred dollars in one of them. Over a hundred dollars!" he exclaimed.

Although there was a certain vagueness to the report, the story did gain widespread circulation at the time. Sometimes the valuables had been found in a "mystery box" and other times they were said to be in a box of books. Depending upon the report, the finder was a housewife, an old man or a young boy. Even the nature of the treasure was shrouded in mystery. It might have been cold, hard cash, land deeds, bank cheques or stock certificates from the depression. In the end, none of this mattered. The important thing was that valuable paper had been secreted in an old book. Father was a believer and mother remained skeptical. She always claimed that such stories had been started by the auctioneers.

Regardless of its origins or validity, the story was enough to convert father to a bibliophile. Paintings were forgotten and books became the new passion. No self respecting prospector would buy a single book because it was easy enough to rifle through the pages and grasp the spine and shake out the leaves. If you were to have any hope, it was necessary to buy the books by the box.

With twelve months in the year, even discounting three or four for bad winter weather, there was still plenty of time for treasure hunting trips. Through a little prior planning and some simple map study, father was able to hit three or four sales in a single day. Ten or twelve trips a year meant that his stockpile began to grow at a prodigious rate. Before long the art gallery was joined by a burgeoning library.

"Johnny, what are we going to do with *all this stuff?*" mother asked.

With his nose buried in a cardboard box of books, father looked up and asked, "What *stuff?*"

Her answer was quick in coming. "The *stuff* in the yard; the *stuff* in the garage; the *stuff* in the attic; the *stuff* hanging on the walls; the *stuff* in the bookcases. The *stuff* that is taking over our living space. *All the stuff* you keep bringing home from those darn auctions."

Father, still on the trail of a stock certificate or currency stash, responded without looking up, "Oh, that stuff."

Exasperated, "Yes that stuff!" mother spat out. "We can't afford a bigger house and the kids are too small to move out. What are we going to do?"

Sensing a brewing storm, father got up, removed two armfuls of books from the couch and squeezed in beside her.

"Well, it does look like a lot of living goes on here. And we're not going to change that. I hope we go on living rich, full lives until we die. These things are 'orphan artifacts' and treasures. We just adopted them until they find their true homes."

Mother broke into a smile at the word 'orphan' and said in a honeyed voice, "'Orphans'. I never thought of them that way. What if I could find a home for the older ones? Stuff we haven't looked at or read for six months or a year? The stuff in the garage and attic. Would that be alright?"

Father thought for a moment and said, "Well, I guess so. If it's in the garage or attic, I guess that's alright."

With a triumphant smile, mother said, "Don't worry about it. Leave the orphans to me."

Now-a-days, yard sales are one of the rituals marking the return of spring. They are ubiquitous. Advertisements fill the back pages of newspapers; hand bills are plastered to lamp posts; homemade signs are stuck on lawns; perched atop family automobiles. So popular has the practice become that the individual entrepreneur has been joined by church groups, civic associations and other charitable organizations.

This wasn't always the case. In the 1950's, coming out of the straightened conditions of the depression and the rationed restrictions of WW II, most people were starting from scratch. They were buying or building houses and beginning families with little or no backup. In the parlance of the stock market, they were <u>buyers</u>, not sellers.

"Well is everybody ready for the auction?" father asked as we finished breakfast. He believed that the early bird *not only got the worm* but also the best bargains.

"Oh, my goodness, I'm afraid I can't go today," Mother said. "I have some chores to do."

This stopped father in his tracks. "What do you mean, you're not going? You always go. It's a *family excursion.*"

"I know dear, I'm awfully sorry," she apologized. "But there are some things I must do. The kids will go with you. They always enjoy the trips."

Now even I had to put my cereal spoon down. This was all brand new territory in our house. First, mother *always* came along just to keep father in line. Second, to say that Suzie and I had a great time was an exaggeration of the highest order. I waited for the second spoon to drop. And then with a dramatic turn, worthy of Alfred Hitchcock, nothing happened. There was only one spoon. Suzie and I were on our way in short order, and as I looked in the rear mirror, I saw mother heading for the garage.

The auction at Essex proved to be a bit of a bust. Father picked through the items with little enthusiasm. Shortly after noon, he suggested we head home. Without mother's company, his heart wasn't in it.

"Won't your mother be surprised when we're back so early?" he asked.

I looked up from the comic I was reading for the *fourth* time. Suzie was slumped over on me, breathing softly. She had the happy faculty of being able to fall asleep at the turn of the ignition key. As a result, she slept through many of the family outings. I envied her.

As we turned off Tecumseh, onto our street, I heard father.

"What the heck is going on? Is somebody having a birthday party or something? Look at all the cars!"

I grabbed onto the back of the seat and craned my neck. Sure enough, the street was lined with cars. People were spilling off a lawn and onto the sidewalk. Even more surprising, it happened to be *our* lawn and *our* sidewalk. Father parked half a block away and walked back towards the milling crowd. Mother was seated at a card table with a pad, pencil and old cigar box in front of her. There was an orderly line of people clutching clothes, books, paintings and assorted household items. On the lawn were two, hand-printed signs that read:

YARD SALE
BOOKS, PAINTINGS, HOUSEHOLD ARTICLES
and "MYSTERY BOXES"

Beside it was another sign with a picture of a diamond ring. The picture had been cut from a magazine. The script read:

LOST
ONE FAMILY RING
LOST AMONG HOUSEHOLD GOODS
PLEASE RETURN TO OWNER
REWARD!

"Hey buddy, where do you think you're going?" said a fat man holding two mystery boxes. "Get to the end of the line and wait like the rest of us."

Father had been trying to make his way to the table. He gave the man a hard look and said, "Excuse me, but that's my wife and I have to talk to her."

The fat fellow gave ground.

"What the heck's going on?" father asked.

Mother smiled as she put a dollar and some change into the cigar box. "I'm helping you out. Don't look so worried dear."

"Helping me out!" he exclaimed. "It looks like you're selling all my stuff!"

In soothing tones, mother answered, "Now you know, I'd never do that. I just cleaned out some stuff from the garage and the attic. I'm trying to find some good homes for your 'orphans'."

Wide-eyed father whispered, "What's all this stuff about a lost ring? That was years ago."

"Oh," mother said, "that's a 'motivator.' I learned it from your auctioneer friends. It's sort of like a masterpiece painting or valuables in a box of books. It seems to be working. I made your favorite pie. Why don't you and the kids go in and have some. I've got more orphans to look after."

Mother's enterprise did not put her in the Guinness Book of Records but it was the *first* yard sale in our neighbourhood. It was also very successful. By popular demand, she held a couple more that summer. As far as I know, no one ever found the "missing ring." Mother didn't seem too concerned but she kept advertising for its return at each sale.

By the end of the summer, our stockpile had dwindled. The Silver Streak was able to return to the shelter of the garage and the attic took on a roomy, almost spacious, appearance. Father still went to auctions but not nearly as often. He said if he couldn't be a collector, he didn't want to be a middle man. He never found a lost masterpiece or hidden stock certificates.

◆   ◆   ◆

A Baby for New Year's
(Sandy Arrives)

Suzie was the first one to notice that there was something the matter with mother. It shouldn't have been a surprise because ever since she had begun kindergarten Suzie had become an expert on illness. Most of her knowledge was based on first hand experience. She had started in September with a cold and then continued her medical journey with the flu, measles, chicken pox, chronic earaches and strep throat. When she came back from the hospital the second time, she told mother she was going to be a nurse because she didn't have the patience to be a patient. Everyone said that was pretty clever for a five year old.

We were playing pick-up-sticks on a blanket in the yard when she said, "There's something wrong with mother."

"What do you mean something's wrong? What kind of something?" I asked.

"Well, I heard her throwing up this morning and it's not the first time."

At eight years old, I knew better than to contradict a budding Florence Nightingale so I said that we should keep our eyes open. Suzie was a real snoop and a bit of a busy body, and I was sure that she would keep both her eyes and ears focused on the situation. A few days later the second shoe dropped, and of course Suzie brought the foot ware to me.

"What does pregnant mean?" she asked.

I could read well, but I had not encountered the word in the Dick and Jane readers.

"Dunno, why are you asking?"

Suzie frowned.

"Well, I heard mother tell father that she might be pregnant. Is it some kind of disease like polio or something?"

At her age, Suzie was getting worried about people dying and what happened to them and all.

"Look, it's not polio. She's walking around and everything; she is not paralyzed. Don't worry. I'll find out what it means."

I said it, but I really didn't know what to do. I couldn't ask mother because if it was a disease she might not want to tell me. If I asked father, he might say "ask mother" because he did that a lot. That's when I decided to follow mother's advice–if you don't know a word, look it up in the dictionary. I headed for the large, family dictionary and sounded it out as best I could.

"Pegnant": no
"Pregant": no again
And finally, "Pregnant":
1) carrying a growing fetus in the uterus
2) Having considerable weight or influence
3) Teeming with ideas
4) Bearing issues or results.

Not much help. It wasn't the first time that I'd gotten the runaround from the dictionary. Sometimes it would substitute one mystery word for another. I read it over the second time, and decided that whatever it was, it didn't sound like polio. I also decided to ask my cousin Donny who was eleven.

"Oh, your mother's going to have a baby. I heard her tell my mother last week."

He was right and soon after that, things started to go crazy in our house. First off, I heard that our tenants upstairs, Mr. and Mrs. Spaulding, were moving out. I decided to ask father about it.

"Mother says the Spauldings are going to move. Is that right?"

"That's right son. They're leaving pretty soon."

"Why do they have to move? I like them. Sometimes they take Suzie and me for a ride. Sometimes they even buy us ice cream."

Father shook his head. "I know you like them. They like you too, but they're leaving next month."

"Aaah, I remember when they drove us around after the tornado and showed us all the broken houses. Father, do you remember that toilet sitting in front of the crushed house?"

One of my earliest memories is watching the black funnel cloud of the Tornado of 1947. It had been hot and sticky all day, but that wasn't unusual for Essex County in the summer. Then the sky turned a peculiar green, and we watched the black swirl come over the flat fields towards our house. Then it turned and veered off to the right. It put down at Walker and Tecumseh roads not far from our house. When it was over, there were thousands of dollars of damages and seventeen people were killed. The Spauldings had a car and took us for a ride to see the damage. The embarrassing picture of that intact creamy white toilet sitting in the front of the ruined remains of the house was seared in memory as a testament to the destructive unpredictability of tornadoes.

"Yes John, I remember the toilet. But the Spauldings have to leave so we can have more room for the baby. I'm going to fix up the upstairs, and you and Suzie will sleep up there."

Holy smoke! What a change. This was big, big, news.

"Do you mean Suzie and I each get our own room after they leave? No more sharing?"

"That's right. You two will move upstairs and the baby will have your room."

In the funny papers they used to draw a little light bulb over a person when they got an idea. Suddenly a light bulb went on and I said, "Father, I really like Mr. Spaulding. I'm going to see if he needs any help with the packing."

As autumn turned into winter, the entire clan was excited about the possibility of a new arrival. Although there were six young women in the family, mother was the only one pregnant at the time. The spotlight was on, and she enjoyed centre stage. I watched with amazement and wonder as she grew, expanded and mushroomed outwards. There was no doubt in my mind that she would need the entire stage.

Of course, everyone in the family pitched in. Soon, used clothes, cradles, baby swings, highchairs, buggies and toys poured in from the uncles and the aunts. Mother said that she recognized some of the stuff because it had belonged to Suzie and me originally. That's the way it was with the clan, everything got shared back and forth. There was no need to be jealous if a cousin got something new because sooner or later, it would come your way. Whatever the article, it was used, reused and used again. By the time my brother, Guy, came along in 1956, some of the things were run down, outdated and in pretty rough shape.

Soon the baby's room was overflowing and some of the stuff started to creep up the stairs to our area and I didn't like that. I told Suzie that she should keep it in her room because then she could help with the baby.

One night at supper mother made a comment that added to the craziness.

"You know the way things are developing, we just might have a Christmas baby."

"Jesus", Father spluttered.

"Not necessarily dear. It might be a girl, you never know."

All of this talk about a baby had generated Suzie's maternal instincts.

"A baby for Christmas, a real baby for Christmas! That would be just like in the Bible. Wait till I tell the kids we're having a baby for Christmas."

"Now take it easy, dear. Babies come when they decide to come. We don't know that it will be Christmas for sure."

Mother's caution didn't make much of an impression. Father began the countdown for a Christmas baby. It was like having a real live advent calendar with a new human being behind the window on the 25th. Suzie began to sort things into two piles: one for a baby brother and one for a sister. She said that she didn't care what it was, but I could tell she was hoping for a boy. She couldn't get that baby Jesus thing out of her mind. Of course, I was excited about Christmas, too. I asked mother if there was a possibility that a bicycle might come along with the baby. She said that she didn't think it would come this year because having a baby was a big expense. I asked about next year. She said we'd have to wait and see. The countdown fizzled out. A Christmas baby didn't arrive. I got a cap gun and two pair of socks. Christmas was a letdown for everybody.

Ever the optimist, father began a new count a few days after Christmas. If we couldn't have a Christmas baby, we would have a New Year's baby instead. Father was really excited about the idea of a New Year's baby. A New Year's baby could be very valuable. Thanks to the local paper and some stores, parents of the first baby born in 1949 would receive valuable gifts as well as cash prizes. This was a real big deal and even I got into the countdown business. After all, there might be prizes for the other kids in the New Year's baby family. Even if there weren't; there might be enough prize money for a bicycle. I began to think that this new baby might work out after all.

Father began to take a real interest in mother's condition. He suggested that they might take a walk every evening after supper and see what happened. Mother said she would be happy to walk as long as he carried the baby. He also thought that some warm baths throughout the day would make her feel better. Mother said that getting in and out of the tub was a real chore, and that he should look after his own bathing needs. For some reason she did seem to be a little crankier than usual. Father said she should try positive thinking. She gave him a funny look, and said that the weight she bore wasn't on her mind. When he suggested a change in diet, mother got kind of short with him. She said that she had done this before, and that the baby would come in its own good time.

New Year's Eve was very quiet. Father said mother should put her feet up in case the baby decided to pop out, and they had to make a run to the hospital. Mother had packed her suitcase. Father had asked a neighbour if he could use the phone for a ride to the hospital. Suzie had filled the bassinet with lots of extra blankets. I had the catalogue opened to the section on bicycles. Everyone was ready except the baby. Suzie and I had some popcorn and ginger ale and went to bed early. Mother rested in bed and father fell asleep in the living room watching the clock. There was no New Year's baby at our house.

Mother had always said that the baby would come whenever it decided. She was right. The baby decided on January 2nd, long after the prizes had been awarded. The thing about babies is that they are so small. It's hard to believe that they could ever grow up and get as big as uncle Clarence. Most of them come out kind of pudgie and wrinkled up like that guy in the newsreels–Winston Churchill. This one was small and sort of like an elf with big, dark eyes. Father smiled and said we would keep her even if she wasn't a New Year's baby. Mother told Suzie not to worry that father was only joking. They called her Sandra Lynn. Now I had two sisters.

Sandy was two when mother initiated the world's first babysitting course and fused the three of us into an unholy alliance.

"Now father and I are going next door to the Edwards. Sandy's asleep, so just be quiet. I'll sit in their side window, Suzie you sit here where you can see me. John, if there's any trouble, run over on the double. There'll be a treat when we get back."

And that's how babysitting 101 began. When father and mother came back after twenty minutes, Suzie and I shared a chocolate bar. It was all so simple and well planned. Had I known where it was all going to lead, I might have packed up and joined the circus that night. After a few more twenty minute visits to the neighbours, mother and father began to stroll around the block. Soon the three of us fell into our assigned roles. Suzie was the mother in training, I was the emergency runner and Sandy was, and remains today, the sleeper in the play. By the time mother and father were going to the Canada Tavern for one beer, Suzie and I had become full fledged babysitters and Sandy was the link that bound us. As I recall, mother did not issue certificates, but there was no question that we had graduated.

As it turned out, the timing of our graduation couldn't have been better. That summer, Chrysler Motors hit upon the plan of shutdowns and layoffs. We could not afford an unpaid vacation so father took the newly acquired Silver Streak back to the farms of his youth. Soon he returned with employment for the whole family.

"We're all going to old man Webster's farm for a few weeks. Your mother and I are going to pick tomatoes, and you three kids can sit on a blanket under the big, old tree. Just enjoy yourself in the shade."

And so began the three longest summers of my life. If Essex County was the sun parlour of Canada and Leamington the Tomato Capital of the Nation, Webster's farm must have been the ponderosa of tomato fields. The rows of plants rolled over the horizon in waves of red. We were adrift on a sea of tomatoes. When I think back on those long, boring summers, I see nothing but red. Suzie and I were old enough to read, write, draw and play board games so if we were bored it must have been our own fault. But sitting on the gray, navy issue blanket, staring at the lines of pickers moving with glacier slowness down the rows, listening to the grass grow around me, I knew better. Knew who to blame. It was all Sandy's fault. Suzie and I wouldn't have been stuck there if it wasn't for our baby sister. Of course it wasn't true, but even at ten I was not one to let facts get in the way of a good prejudice.

If life was hard on the baby sitters, it was a thousand times worse for mother and father. They would start early when the dew was still on the grass trying to beat the summer heat. But, there was no beating the summer heat in Essex County. By noon, the July and August sun would bake and crack the earth between the rows and the bigger tomatoes would split. Mother and father would come back to the blanket under the elm tree for lunch. Lunch was a simple matter because it was all around us. Unlike the poet who had a loaf of bread, a jug of wine and his lover, we had bread, water, tomatoes and each other. Not exactly the same.

Some pickers would take a rest after lunch, but not them. Father said there was no money in resting. They would start at opposite ends of neighbouring rows and walk towards the middle. Father would keep count of the baskets and lug the full bushels to the pick-up area. I was the water boy, and at a signal, I would run the jug down to where they were working. It was hard, sweaty and fatiguing work that went from early morning to the onset of the evening. At last, bone tired, they would finish the count, gather up some tomatoes, and head for home. All five of us knew what the morrow would bring. More of the same.

Father found a positive even in the midst of misery.

"You know one of the advantages of this job is that you can take the food home with you. That is what I call a bonus."

Father was not an executive; he worked on the line, and so his concept of a bonus was far different from that of a modern CEO. I understood what he was saying, but I figured if that was the way you picked a job, we should all work in a chocolate bar or potato chip factory. I guess I was the only one who couldn't see the benefits of the situation. Father packed half a basket of tomatoes in the trunk every night and mother got out grandmother's Women's Institute Cookbook.

That was the summer I discovered the many possibilities of tomatoes as a food source. Out in the field we had tomato sandwiches for lunch but I soon realized that was a common and pedestrian use of this fruit/vegetable. Mother got to work crushing, smashing and mashing the little red devils. With some help from other vegetables, you could have all kinds of soups, and we did. There was tomato and celery, tomato and carrot, tomato and potato, and of course, the good old fashioned tomato and milk. If it was too hot for soup in the summer, and it was, you could have it cold. As mother said, there were endless possibilities for a good soup.

The cookbook also presented a variety of methods for the preparation of tomatoes. I blame the diet for the nightmares. I was eating tomatoes three meals a day and the tomatoes knew it. The dream began as a happy Broadway musical. Dressed a la Fred Astaire in a flashy red Tuxedo, with green cane and a tall tomato crown, I was surrounded by a circle of small, smiling tomatoes. They were singing "You're the King, You're the King". I began a soft shoe shuffle, the mood changed from happy dancing tomatoes to menacing blood, red ketchup. The tomatoes became large and angry, and they closed the circle around me. At this point, ugly, fat, horned tomato worms began sliding down from my tomato crown. At four or five inches, the green horned tomato worm consistently wins the title of the world's ugliest caterpillar; in my nightmare they were the size of pythons. At the age of five, I had helped father picking and squishing the invaders in our garden. Now it was payback time. Would I ever get out of the Webster's red hell and off the tomato diet?

Near the end of the second summer we began a game of the imagination. It didn't end the boredom; nothing could do that. It just put a different slant on things.

I asked Suzie, "What would you do right now, if you were at home?"

"That's easy. I would skip rope with my girlfriends. What would you do?"

I had gotten a bike and I said, "Oh, I would ride to Bucky's and we would play baseball."

Ever in the mothering mode, Suzie asked "What would you do Sandy, if you were at home?"

"Wanna go home. Wanna go home," was the reply.

We resumed the game in the third summer, but we competed to make our answer more outlandish. I was going to pitch for the Tigers, or walk to California to visit my aunt or climb a mountain in Africa. Suzie imagined that she might discover a cure for polio, join a circus or become a ballerina. Sandy's answer was always the same. "Wanna go home, wanna go home."

At the beginning of the fourth summer father said that since Sandy was four, we could take her into the woods and pick hickory and walnuts. We would store them in the garage and they would be good for Christmas.

They say it is the highest apple in the tree that looks best. It's the same with walnuts. Suzie said she would go up and throw the nuts down. I would help Sandy collect them and put them in the bag. Jokingly, I said I would catch her if she fell. She did but I didn't. I told her that the ankle wasn't broken because she could still stand on it and sort of walk.

It was late by the time we made it back to the elm tree. Suzie limped all the way and the ankle grew bigger and bigger. Using his naval first aid, father said there was no break, just a bad sprain. Mother said the whole thing was getting out of hand. Sandy balled up her fists and began to wail, "Wanna go home, wanna go home, wanna go home."

Mother always said that Sandy was father's favorite because she was almost a New Year's baby.

Father turned away from the weeping and wailing and said, "You're right. Can't stand to see the little one suffer. I'll tell Webster we're finished at the end of the week."

The crying stopped. My baby sister looked up at me and gave me a broad wink. Imagine a wink from a five year old. The wink said it all. The wink said we're out of here and I've loved her ever since.

◆   ◆   ◆

Mother Gets a Job

Throughout history, dinners have proven to be significant turning points. There was the case of Ulysses and his Greek gyros which featured a wooden horse as the main course and Count Metternick who hosted a banquet in Vienna as he carved up Europe. The practice continues today at the UN conferences and G8 meetings which highlight concluding summaries at the final banquets.

This sort of thing never happened at our house–at least not until "the employment incident" raised its ugly head. Father said 'messing time' was part of regular duty hour. It was a time for eating, not idle chatter. Conversation was confined to sustenance necessities such as "please pass the bread," or "is there anymore soup?" As captain of our ship, he commanded proceedings from the head of the table. We ate at 17:30 and were finished in time for the radio news at 18:00 hours. This was no mere routine but standard operating procedure.

All of this changed on a memorable Saturday night in 1952. After she had served the family dessert, mother took her place at the far end of the table and said that she had some important news. She announced that she had been doing a lot of thinking and had decided that it was time she got a job.

I couldn't have been more surprised if she had told us aliens had landed a flying saucer in the backyard, and we all had fifteen minutes to pack. With his mouth half full of Jell-o, father was at a loss for words. There was a moment of complete, total, funereal silence in which you could have heard a spoon drop at Bobby G's, a half-block away.

At last father broke the eerie stillness and asked, "What do you mean 'a job'?"

Mother's response was as quick and fiery as a Roman candle on Victoria Day.

"You know? A job. A position of employment. A work-for-pay activity. An occupation. A paying situation. A job."

Father, the ex-navy man, was once again at sea. After a not so pregnant pause, he responded, "I don't understand. You've already got a job. Right here. You've got the kids to look after and all the stuff around the house. There's plenty to keep you busy right here."

"No. What I have here is drudgery. On Monday morning I'm going downtown to look for employment. My mind is made up."

And with that, she dipped into her Jell-O while father fixed a concentrated stare on the teapot. Unfortunately she had already cleared away the cutlery because we could have used a knife, or two, to cut through the silence. Had there been aliens with a flying saucer in the backyard, I would have been more than willing to climb aboard.

We didn't hear anymore about "the job" for the rest of the weekend. In fact, all conversation was kept to a cold, frosty and bare minimum. I was more than ready for school on Monday morning

It was the middle of the week when the second shoe dropped, with a thud.

This time mother waited until after supper, and then she said, "You'll have to keep an eye on the kids this Saturday. I'm going downtown to Smith's department store."

Still hoping for the best, father asked, "What's going on at Smith's? Is there a big sale or something?"

"No. I'm going for a job interview. I don't know how long I'll be gone."

Father's response hung in the air like a limp flag at half mast.

Finally he said, "Oh."

The next Saturday morning Suzie and I watched as mother got ready to go to the city. She was dressed in her good, black dress–the one for weddings and funerals. Her black, high heels were shining like newly cut coal and she was wearing her Sunday pill-box hat (but without the veil). Her hair was swept up, and she was wearing lipstick. I noticed her studying some notes on her recipe cards before she put them in her small handbag. She looked professional, just like one of my teachers. She looked *good*. In fact, she looked *very good*. She just didn't look like *my* mother.

As she left, she called over her shoulder, "I'm not sure how long this will take. There's a casserole in the fridge, and you can put it in the oven at 375 degrees, if I'm not back by 5 o'clock."

With that, the new professional swept out of our house and headed for the bus stop. We were pretty certain that her instructions were for our father, but things were changing so fast, who could be sure? Our mouths were wide open, as if prepared for a fly-swallowing contest, as we watched her stride down the driveway.

She was back early in the afternoon so father didn't have to tackle the casserole. Suzie and I were glad because we remembered the time he tried to make pancakes for Mother's Day. Most of them came out in the shape of small automobile tires (with the same colour and rubbery texture). Suzie called them 'baby wheels.' Mother said it was a nice idea, but maybe we could pass on breakfast and have brunch somewhere.

She came clip-clopping into the house, and we were all relieved. When father asked how it had gone, she said her shoes were killing her. She would tell us about it once she changed her clothes. When she reappeared, we all sat around the kitchen table and mother and father had, what they called, a "discussion." As I listened to the back and forth, it seemed more like a tennis match.

Father served first.

"I'm not happy about this. I don't know why you have to get a job? Things are good at the plant and we have enough money."

Mother's return had a bit of a spin to it.

"It's not about the money. The money has nothing to do with it," she remarked.

Father's return was weak, and left him wide open.

"I don't get it," he said. "None of the neighbours' wives have jobs. Why do you need one?"

"This isn't about the neighbours either. As you always tell the kids, 'if the neighbours jumped off the Ambassador Bridge, would you jump too?' I want the job for *me*, not the neighbours. And not for the money."

It was true. The bridge metaphor was one of my parents' favorite arguments. They both used it, but I recall that mother was more partial to it. As a kid, I had seen the Ambassador Bridge many times, and I had no desire to leap from the top. On the other hand, the idea did hold a certain fascination. If all the people in Windsor started jumping, I hoped that I would be there to watch. I would later learn that this is what philosophers call a theoretical position and, as such, a weak tactic. While that might have been true in Philosophy 101, the "jumping off the bridge" argument was well used at our house. I had never been able to win against it. Neither was father.

Father snorted. He knew better than to try to cross that bridge. Instead, he launched into a series of questions.

"What about the kids? Who will look after things around the house? What about the cooking and cleaning? Who's going to do that if you get a job?"

These were good questions but, once again, mother was prepared. She fired the ball right back.

She said, "It won't be every day. Besides, you're at work and the kids are at school all day. Everybody's got some place to be, and I might as well be some place too."

Whomp! Game, set, match. I gave the game to mother based on her energy and determination. Then again, as far as the job issue was concerned, she was playing on her own court. That might have been the end of round two but, it certainly wasn't the end of the "debate." The job business began to resemble United Nations' meetings. I began to long for the "good old days" of naval silence at meal time.

Father wondered what would happen to Suzie and me if mother was working. And who would look after the house while she was gone? Mother said that we were at school all day and father would be home before us on weekdays, plus all day Saturday. She would only be working Thursday through Saturday. As for the house, she thought it could stand on its own while we were all out during the day.

And so the debates continued. After awhile there were no new arguments, but that didn't end the "discussions."

The next act in our domestic drama occurred at the beginning of the week. When we got home from school, the table was spread with a linen table cloth and the good company dishes and silverware. A vase with a small yellow rose served as a centre piece. The aroma of chicken wafted through the kitchen like a refreshing morning mist. If I had not just returned from school, I would have thought it was Sunday dinner. There was even a cold bottle of beer at father's place, which was unusual since it wasn't his birthday or anything. I was certain that something big was in the air-besides the smell of chicken.

Mother was so excited she couldn't even wait for the carving.

As soon as we all sat down, she began, "I had some good news today. I thought we should celebrate. The store called and I'm to start training and work this Thursday. Isn't that great?"

No one said a word; although father took a long, hard pull at his beer. Suddenly Suzie burst into tears and asked mother if she was moving away. Mother told us no. She said that going to work was just like us going to school. She would be home every night and in the morning when we left for the day.

Once Suzie settled down, I asked mother what she would be doing at the store. She said she wasn't sure but that she might be operating an elevator. I said that sounded pretty cool. Father said he hoped she wouldn't run over anyone and asked whether there were any more potatoes. Except for Suzie's outburst, it was one of the quietest celebrations I had ever attended.

When I was four or five years old, a tornado struck Windsor. Of course the upheaval in our household was not equal in proportion; but mother's new career did trigger some major adjustments. After awhile, father mastered the oven temperature controls and the casseroles turned from charred ebony to a muddy brown. Mother seemed unable to see the dirty dishes as they piled in the sink and on the counter. Finally, when we ran out of plates and cutlery, father assigned us kids to "clean-up" duty. Suzie washed while I dried and put away. When I complained about all the soups and sandwiches, mother brought a cookbook from the library. The attractive cover bore a picture of two happy children at work in the kitchen. It was called "Cooking for Kids" and, although I never did read it, some of the pictures were very tempting.

As for mother, she took to elevator operation as if she was flying for Trans Canada Airlines. It was like she discovered her Shangri-la in an elevator.

Mother had been working for three weeks, and things had settled down on the home front. Then father suggested the three of us go downtown on Saturday. We didn't usually go to the city unless it was market day or Christmas. Christmas was still three months away, and father said we weren't going to the market. None of that mattered to me or Suzie. We were going to the city and excited about the trip. We got out at the central bus terminal, and a two block walk brought us to the entrance to Smith's department store.

Father smiled and said, "Well, let's go in and see what's on sale today."

Suzie and I bolted for the revolving door and twirled our way inside. Smith's was the biggest department store in the city. It attracted people from both sides of the river. There were already many people in the entrance when Suzie said she wanted to see the toys. Father said we could take the elevator and get directions. Mother was surprised to see us, but she recovered quickly and said that the toys were on the fourth floor. We stepped in and watched "the professional" in action.

"Watch your step and please step right back," she said. Glancing out to the left and right she called, "Elevator going up. Anyone else for the elevator? Stand clear while I close both doors. Thank you."

With that, she touched a button and the heavy door closed. Carefully, she slid the grated metal door in place and pushed the throttle away from her. Suzie watched with gigantic bug eyes. Using the elevator was almost as exciting as riding in the aliens' flying saucer.

When we reached the second floor, mother made sure the elevator was flush to the floor and then reversed the door closing process.

"Please watch your step," she cautioned. "This is the second floor with furniture, carpets and draperies. Thank you for shopping with us and enjoy your day at Smith's. This is the second floor and the elevator is going up. Anyone else for the elevator? Stand clear while I close the doors."

It was a simple job. One which in a few years, would become automated and customer operated. But we could tell that mother enjoyed the people she met. With hands on the controls and one eye on the floor gauge, she smiled and chatted with everyone. She seemed to know a lot about the store and the surrounding shops, restaurants and theatres. Anyone could tell she was happy in her work and took pride in doing her job well. It wasn't brain surgery but it was mother's ticket to a world outside our house.

As we exited the elevator, a tall man turned to father and said, "That's a good looking woman and she knows what she's doing."

Beaming back, father answered, "You're right about that. She sure is and she sure does."

Chapter VII

Coming of Age-The Tigers and Me

I would have exited the turnstiles of childhood eventually-we all do-
,but I believe that the 1952 Detroit Tigers speeded up the process.

◆　　　◆　　　◆

The Tigers and Me

It was the radio that told me Babe Ruth had died. It was August 13,
1948. Father and I were in the living room listening to the baseball
game when the announcer broke in with the news. The Bambino, the
Sultan of Swat, the man who saved baseball and put Yankee Stadium
on the map, was dead.

"Well, he's gone," Father said. "Been sick for quite awhile. It will
be a long time before we see his like again."

I looked over and asked, "Did you ever see him play?"

He smiled and said, "Many, many times."

Now I was intrigued.   Father was a big baseball fan. He followed
the Tigers not the Yankees because Detroit was only a mile wide river
from Windsor, Ontario.

"Did you go to New York or did you see him play in Detroit?"

His smile broadened, "Neither son." He tapped his temple and
said, "Sometimes I saw him at home, sometimes on a ship in Halifax,
in a bar or at the beach. You see, I saw him on the radio."

"Oh. I thought you saw him in real life."

Father laughed. "But I did see him in real life. Right here in my
imagination," and he tapped his head again. "I knew what the Babe
looked like from the papers and the news reels. I could see him trotting

'round the bases—a plump little ham on spindly chicken legs. Yeah, thanks to the radio, I saw him many times."

"So what will happen to baseball now that he is dead?" I asked.

Father gave me a long look and said, "What do you mean 'what will happen to baseball?' It will go on. They will dim the lights, lower the flags, say a few words and then they will yell, 'Play Ball.' That's the way baseball is."

As I grew up I realized that was the beauty of the game. Come floods or tornadoes, good times or bad, depression or world wars, health, sickness, or even death, baseball would go on. It had a life of its own and was bigger than any one man. It was bigger than all of us. Oh sure, winter might stop it for a few months, but come spring, baseball would return with the same certainty as the robins and daffodils. Like new flowers bursting forth and blooming in the garden, there would be new players and new games, but there would be the same old baseball.

Father was right about the radio and baseball, too. Baseball was always connected to the radio. In my childhood the two were tied as closely as the pitcher to the ball and the hitter to his bat. Baseball was a living, breathing entity, and the radio was the vehicle of delivery. As a child sitting beside my father, I listened to the game as evening came on. The crickets echoed the announcer's commentary, and somewhere a garden hose refreshed a lawn. Still later, the sounds would waft up as I settled into bed. Even now I sometimes hear them just before sleep—"two on, two out and the pitchers coming to bat."

On weekends, the afternoon game resounded up and down our street. Men washing cars, trimming hedges, doing odd jobs to the call of a radio tucked into an open window. Sometimes you could walk the length of the street and never be beyond the sound of the game. The game and the afternoon seemed to stretch on forever. It was Saturday, and no one was in a hurry. Baseball was the slow and lazy river down which you could float at ease, adrift in time's stream. The slow moving, never ending Saturday was as permanent as nine innings and twenty seven outs. The pitcher wound up, the batter stared out and time stood still.

Father must have had a built in antenna, finely tuned to the radio and baseball. After working in the garden, he would stretch out on the couch and listen to the game. Flat on his back, eyes closed and hands clasped over his chest, he looked like he was posing for a photo at a funeral home. Actually, the announcer's voice had carried him back to Brigg's Stadium. He was perched halfway up in the second tier between home plate and first base. Not the best or most expensive seat, but at least he wasn't behind one of the poles, common in the old park. As the game progressed, he would relax until at last a gentle snore would ruffle his pursed lips. Mother would give him five minutes, and then slip in and turn off the radio.

With the suddenness of a hard hit grounder streaking between short and second, his eyes would fly open and he would demand, "Why did you turn it off? I was listening to the game."

Caught in the act, mother would respond, "You certainly were not. The whole house could hear you snoring."

"I was just breathing deeply. There were two on and two out and could you please turn it back on?"

Mother had no idea and less interest in what 'two on two out' might mean; she would switch it back on, and head for the kitchen. Father would allow himself a small satisfied smile and return to his reverie. I don't believe there were always two on and two out, but that was his standard line. After all, it sounded so important that death itself couldn't drag you away at that juncture.

Years later, Yogi Berra gained baseball immortality for his statement that "it was never over until it was over." Father preceded him in part with his standard line to mother, "Leave it on, it ain't over yet."

◆   ◆   ◆

I was ten years old when I discovered that baseball and radio were not the total magic I had imagined. My cousin and I were listening to a Tiger versus Yankee game, and as usual, I was enchanted by the announcer's call.

I turned to Donny and said, "Wouldn't it be great to be an announcer, and go to all those cities and see all those games?"

He looked at me with the wisdom of a fourteen year old and said, "He doesn't go to all the games. They're playing in New York and he's in Detroit."

I no longer believed in Santa Claus and the Easter Bunny and I wasn't about to be taken in by another tall tale.

"That's baloney! What do you take me for, a stupid kid? How can he call a game if he's not even there?"

Then Donny revealed the first of baseball's deceits.

"He gets the stuff by teletype. It comes into the station on a typewriter and he reads it."

"You're crazy! What about the short stop scooting to his left or the right fielder climbing the wall for a one handed catch? What about all that stuff?"

With a shake of his head, he said, "Well he already knows what happened. He just describes it so it's exciting."

"You mean he makes it all up?"

"Well, I guess he does a bit. If you don't believe me, listen and you'll hear the machine clicking in the background."

He was right. I could hear the clicking and it took some of the shine off the ball. In the past, the announcer's dramatic descriptions had painted a vivid and lively picture of the game's action. There were no passive verbs in the radio commentary. Even when the pitcher held the ball and stared in at the batter, the announcer outlined the options and possibilities in breathless detail. The stoppage became a time of tension. You felt the pitcher's strangled swallow and the hitter's iron lock on the bat handle. And you waited. Always there was the electrifying excitement as the high inside buzz ball whizzed past the batter's ear or the Texas leaguer fell safely between outfielders, and best of all, the 'going, going gone' of the homerun. These were the thrilling sounds of baseball. Of course, I still listened, but now I couldn't get that clicking out of my head.

◆   ◆   ◆

The next year I got to see my first game in person and for awhile, I forgot my previous disappointments. With forty five other noisy and excited safety patrollers, I was bussed through the tunnel and dropped at Brigg's Stadium – the home of the Detroit Tigers. Over the years downtown Detroit had acquired a notorious reputation as a centre for crime and violence, and I was probably one of the very few humans who saw it as the site of a holy shrine.

After standing in line for twenty minutes, we were led into the stadium and deposited like a mammoth homerun – high up and far out in right field. It was a night game, and we were near the top of the stadium. The coal black sky hung all about us, but the strong stadium lights bathed the billiard green field in a golden hue. As I gazed down, I was reminded of my mother's jewelry box which lit up when you opened the lid. Below me was the golden diamond and perched high in the nosebleed section on a hard, wooden green coloured seat, I knew I was in Olympus.

All around me, the other kids scuffled, shoved and squirmed in and out of their seats. Excited and boisterous they were like a bunch of monkeys let loose in banana factory. From the comments around me, I could tell that not everyone shared my passion for the game.

"Cheeze, that was a long way up!"

"Yeh, I never thought we'd stop climbing. This section must be reserved for kids and mountain goats."

"Is that the field down there? Man, it's a long way down."

"Yeh, I thought the players would be bigger. They look like a bunch of ants."

"Hey, it looks like they're practicing. I thought they were professionals and knew how to play."

"Yeh! Let's get something to eat before the game starts. This is boring."

As for me, I was hypnotized by the warm ups. The coaches' batted long fly balls to the outfielders who loped across the field with the grace of white tailed deer and gathered the balls into their gloves with the ease of apple pickers at harvest time. They slashed fungoes to the infielders who scooped and fired them back like well oiled robots. The players went through the warm ups with effortless precision; they made it all look so easy, but I knew that it wasn't. Anyone could see that these Tigers would be hard to beat.

I poured over my orange and blue program with the snarling tiger on the cover. There was an official scorecard inside so I didn't have to draw one up from my school scribbler. Like a pilot receiving instructions from the tower, I hung on the words of the PA announcer, and inscribed the names into the scorecard. One name stood out from the rest, and I printed it in large, capital, block letters. The Tigers had a new catcher and his name was Matt Batts! For me, it was a classic baseball name, and the fact that he was a catcher made it all the more appropriate. I imagined writing a sport series with Matt as the hero.

Matt Batts and the Little League,
Matt Batts Goes to College,
Matt Batts and the Terrific Tigers,

and finally

Matt Batts – World Series Hero.

The titles alone would guarantee success. In truth, Matt was a journeyman catcher who played for five teams in both leagues in ten years, but he was a Tiger with a big league name.

The Tigers lost to the Indians that night, but it didn't matter because I was there. I would have been willing to stay all night in the darkened stadium and walk home. I would have been willing, but I didn't.

I didn't see another game but I followed all of them on the radio. I reproduced the official scorecard into my school scribbler and made copies for each game. I clipped and saved box scores from the newspapers and compared them with my scorecards. After the game at the stadium, I began a Tiger scrapbook with newspaper articles. I was hooked as deeply as my father. I was one with the Tiger Team, and had become a baseball fan-natic.

Youth is a time of optimism and hope, and with the 1952 Tigers you needed large doses of both. I knew that they were losing a lot of games but the announcers, Van Patrick and others, seemed to make it close and interesting. Father said that they were paid cheerleaders, but I didn't want to believe him. As the season progressed, they fell further and further behind the other teams. The pitcher became the manager and a trading frenzy developed as old players left and new ones arrived. The announcers said that the team was building for their future. I was young; I could wait; but as one loss followed another, I began to wonder how long it would be. Finally I developed two life-long goals. I must live long enough to see Halley's come by and the Tigers win the World Series. I knew the comet was scheduled for 1985 but I wasn't sure about the Tigers.

It was the end of the season, and Father said we should review the year's statistics.

"Let's see what their final record looks like. I don't think it's very good."

It wasn't; the Tigers had finished a very dead last for the first time in their history. They had 50 wins and 104 losses; it would be over fifty years before a Tiger team would lose more.

I was mystified.

"How could Virgil Trucks pitch two no hitters and a one hitter and only win five games?"

"Well son, like they say, it's a team game. Besides, look on the bright side; he lost nineteen, and you gotta be a good pitcher to lose that many."

He was right; it was a team effort. My favorite, Matt Batts, mirrored his teammates and batted only .237 with 3 homers and 13 R.B.I. But at least he didn't change his name.

I would have exited through the turnstiles of childhood eventually - we all do - but I think that the 1952 Tigers speeded up the process. I still listened and scored but now I knew that the announcers painted favorable pictures from the teletyped copy. I also knew that the Tigers were not a great team; in fact they weren't even a good team. Players would come and go, and no one would be a Tiger forever. Baseball had made me a little more critical and a lot more mature.

As Father had said about Babe Ruth, baseball would be there long after we were gone.

The next year Matt Batts became the regular catcher and hit .278.

One year later, I left Victoria elementary and entered high school. It was time for me to play in a different league.

◆   ◆   ◆

Conclusion

In April 1995 I lost my best friend when my sister Sib (Sylvia) died after long and heroic struggles with cancer. Whether hiking, swimming or sharing a conversation or a sunset, she has lived with me daily. I hope through these stories of Suzie others may come to know her as well.

John and Mabel celebrated their sixtieth wedding anniversary at the Canadian Legion in Kingsville on June 24, 2000. It was a festive occasion with friends and family–their brothers, sisters, children, nieces, nephews, grandchildren and great grands. Glancing around the crowded hall, I was amazed at what two people could create when they set their minds to it. Within a year we were back in Kingsville to arrange my father's funeral; mother followed between Christmas and New Year's in 2005. Ten days before she and I shared a quiet pre-Christmas breakfast and laughed over the year of the duplicate Christmas presents, the little tree built from scratch and the later one that was too big to fit through the back door. Increased affluence brought a different set of problems.

Neither of my parents went beyond elementary school but they emphasized the importance of education. When she died Sylvia was a manager at Manufacturer's Life, Sandy is a nurse in the I.T. department at St. Joseph's hospital in London, Guy is an executive with the Alberta Research Council and I have retired from a career of teaching and administration. Who can deny the power of the media? Growing up in the fifties, we were saturated with televisions idealized visions of suburban, middle-class families. It shaped our lives.

For better or worse, we all ended up living next door to the Cleavers.